# BRIGHT NOTES

# HENRY V BY WILLIAM SHAKESPEARE

## Intelligent Education

Nashville, Tennessee

BRIGHT NOTES: Henry V
www.BrightNotes.com

No part of this publication may be used or reproduced in any manner whatsoever without written permission, except in the case of brief quotations in critical articles and reviews. For permissions, contact Influence Publishers http://www.influencepublishers.com.

ISBN: 978-1-645425-64-9 (Paperback)
ISBN: 978-1-645425-65-6 (eBook)

Published in accordance with the U.S. Copyright Office Orphan Works and Mass Digitization report of the register of copyrights, June 2015.

Originally published by Monarch Press.
Laura Lippman, 1964
2020 Edition published by Influence Publishers.

Interior design by Lapiz Digital Services. Cover Design by Thinkpen Designs.

Printed in the United States of America.

Library of Congress Cataloging-in-Publication Data forthcoming.
Names: Intelligent Education
Title: BRIGHT NOTES: Henry V
Subject: STU004000 STUDY AIDS / Book Notes

# CONTENTS

| | | |
|---|---|---|
| 1) | Introduction to William Shakespeare | 1 |
| 2) | Introduction to Henry V | 6 |
| 3) | Textual Analysis | |
| | Act 1 | 11 |
| | Act 2 | 29 |
| | Act 3 | 48 |
| | Act 4 | 72 |
| | Act 5 | 98 |
| 4) | Character Analyses | 110 |
| 5) | Critical Commentary | 126 |
| 6) | Essay Questions and Answers | 133 |
| 7) | Subject Bibliography and Guide to Research Papers | 140 |
| 8) | General Biography and Criticism | 143 |

# INTRODUCTION TO WILLIAM SHAKESPEARE

On April 26, 1564, William Shakespeare, son of John Shakespeare and Mary Arden, was christened in Holy Trinity Church, Stratford-on-Avon. His birthday is traditionally placed three days before. He was the eldest of four boys and two girls born to his father, a well-to-do glover and trader, who also held some minor offices in the town government. He probably attended the local free school, where he picked up the "small Latin and less Greek" that Ben Jonson credits him with. ("Small" Latin to that knowledgeable classicist meant considerably more than it does today.) As far as is known, this was the extent of Shakespeare's formal education. In November of 1582, when he was eighteen, a license was issued for his marriage to Ann Hathaway, a Stratford neighbor eight years older than himself. The following May their child Susanna was christened in the same church as her father. While it may be inferred from this that his marriage was a forced one, such an inference is not necessary; engagement at that time was a legally binding contract and was sometimes construed as allowing conjugal rights. Their union produced two more children, twins Judith and Hamnet, christened in February, 1585. Shortly thereafter Shakespeare left Stratford for a career in London. What he did during these years - until we pick him up, an established playwright, in 1592 - we do not know, as no records exist. It is presumed that he served an apprenticeship in the theatre, perhaps as a provincial trouper, and eventually won himself a place as an actor. By 1594 he was a successful dramatist with the Lord Chamberlain's company (acting groups had noble protection and patronage), having produced the *Comedy of Errors* and the *Henry VI* trilogy, probably in collaboration with older, better established dramatists. When the plague closed the London theatres for many months of 1593-94, he found himself without a livelihood. He promptly turned his hand to poetry (although written in verse, plays were not considered as dignified as poetry), writing two long narrative poems, *Venus and Adonis* and *The Rape of Lucrece*. He dedicated them to the Earl of Southampton, undoubtedly receiving some recompense. The early nineties also saw the first of Shakespeare's **sonnets** circulating in manuscript, and later finding their way into print. In his early plays - mostly chronicle histories glorifying England's past, and light comedies - Shakespeare sought for popular success and achieved it. In 1599 he was able to buy a share in the Globe Theatre, where he acted and where his plays were performed. His ever-increasing financial success enabled him to buy a good deal of real estate in his native Stratford, and by 1605 he was able to retire from acting. Shortly thereafter he began to spend most of his time in Stratford, to which he retired around 1610. Very little is known of his life after he left London. He died on April 23, 1616, in Stratford, and was buried there. In 1623 the *First Folio* edition of his complete works was published by a group of his friends as a testimonial to his memory. This was a very rare tribute, because at the time plays were generally considered to be inferior literature, not really worthy of publication. These scanty facts, together with some information about the dates of his plays, are all that is definitely known about the greatest writer in the history of English literature. The age in which Shakespeare lived was not as concerned with keeping accurate records as we are, and any further details about Shakespeare's life have been derived from educated guesses based on knowledge of his time. Shakespeare's plays fall into three major groups according to the periods in his development when he wrote them:

## EARLY COMEDIES AND HISTORIES

The first group consists of romantic comedies such as *A Midsummer Night's Dream* (1593-5), and of strongly patriotic histories such as *Henry V* (1599). The early comedies are full of farce and slapstick, as well as exuberant poetry. Their plots are complicated and generally revolve around a young love relationship. The histories are typical of the robust, adventurous English patriotism of the Elizabethan era, when England had achieved a position of world dominance and power.

## THE GREAT TRAGEDIES

The second period, beginning with *Hamlet* and ending with *Antony and Cleopatra,* is the period of the great tragedies: *Hamlet* (1602); *Othello* (1604); *King Lear* (1605); *Macbeth* (1606); and *Antony and Cleopatra* (1607-8). Shakespeare seems to have gone through a mental crisis at this time. His vision of the world darkens, and he sees life as an **epic** battle between the forces of good and evil, between order and chaos within man and in the whole universe. The forces for good win out in the end over evil, which is self-defeating. But the victory of the good is at great cost and often comes at the point of death. It is a moral victory, not a material one. These tragedies center on a great man who, because of some flaw in his makeup, or some error he commits, brings death and destruction down upon himself and those around him. They are generally considered the greatest of Shakespeare's plays.

## THE LATE ROMANCES

In the third period Shakespeare returns to romantic comedy. But such plays as *Cymbeline* (1609-10), *The Winter's Tale* (1610-11), and *The Tempest* (1611) are very different in point of view and structure from such earlier comedies as *Much Ado About Nothing* (1599) and *Twelfth Night* (1600). Each of these late romances has a situation potentially tragic, and there is much bitterness in them. Thus the destructive force of insane jealousy serves as the **theme** both of the tragedy, *Othello*, and the comedy, *The Winter's Tale*. They are serious comedies, replacing farce and slapstick with rich symbolism and supernatural events. They deal with such **themes** as sin and redemption, death and rebirth, and the conflict between nature and society, rather than with simple romantic love. In a sense they are deeply religious, although unconnected with any church dogma. In his last play, *The Tempest,* Shakespeare achieved a more or less serene outlook upon the world after the storm and stress of his great tragedies and the so-called "dark comedies."

## SHAKESPEARE'S THEATRE

Shakespeare's plays were written for a stage very different from our own. Women, for instance, were not allowed to act; so female parts, even that of Cleopatra, were played by boy actors whose voices had not yet changed. The plays were performed on a long platform surrounded by a circular, unroofed theatre, and were dependent on natural daylight for lighting. There was no curtain separating the stage from the audience, nor were there act divisions. These were added to the plays by later editors. Because the stage jutted right into the audience, Shakespeare was able to achieve a greater intimacy with his spectators than modern playwrights can. The audience in the pit, immediately surrounding the stage, had to stand crowded together throughout the play. Its members tended to be lower class Londoners who would frequently comment aloud on the action of the play and break into fights. Anyone who attended the plays in the pit did so at the risk of having his pockets picked, of catching a disease, or, at best, of being jostled about by the crude "groundlings." The aristocratic and merchant classes, who watched the plays from seats in the galleries, were spared most of the physical discomforts of the pit.

## ITS ADVANTAGES

There were certain advantages, however, to such a theatre. Because complicated scenic, lighting and sound effects were impossible, the playwright had to rely on the power of his words to create scenes in the audience's imagination. The rapid changes of scene and vast distances involved in *Antony and Cleopatra*, for instance, although they create a problem for modern producers, did not for Shakespeare. Shakespeare did not rely - as the modern realistic theatre does - on elaborate stage scenery to create atmosphere and locale. For these, as for battle scenes involving large numbers of people, Shakespeare relied on the suggestive power of his poetry to quicken the imagination of his audience. Elizabethan audiences were very lively anyway, and quick to catch any kind of word play. Puns, jokes, and subtle poetic effects made a greater impression on them than on modern audiences, who are less alert to language.

# INTRODUCTION TO HENRY V

## IMMEDIATE SOURCES FOR HENRY V

Shakespeare's primary source seems to have been Holinshed's *Chronicles* (1578), for many passages in the play are very similar to those in Holinshed. But Holinshed himself drew heavily on Hall's *Union of the Two Noble Houses of Lancaster and York* (1548), and, therefore, it is not always possible to tell where Shakespeare is following Hall and where Holinshed. Other sources available to Shakespeare were the Gesta, written by a chaplain who accompanied Henry to France and a biography called the Vita et Gesta Henrici Quinti, written by an unknown author about thirty years after the death of Henry. It is also possible that Shakespeare may have seen other chronicles, including the account of the Frenchman Le Fevre. Plays about Henry V had been written before this one, but it is impossible to say how much Shakespeare may have borrowed from them. The only earlier play extant is the *Famous Victories of Henry V,* which was registered in 1594. It is believed that an earlier version of this play has been lost. In any case, Shakespeare's *Henry V* bears only superficial resemblance to the *Famous Victories.*

## THE TEXT OF HENRY V

Shakespeare's plays were at times published without his consent during his lifetime, and pirated and generally inaccurate versions resulted. Thus in 1600 a bad Quarto edition of *Henry V* appeared, based on the recollections of actors in the play. In 1623, however, Shakespeare's friends put out a Folio edition of his plays derived from his own manuscripts. Our modern text is based on the 1623 folio.

## BRIEF SUMMARY OF HENRY V

The main action of the play is concerned with the historical events leading up to and following the battle of Agincourt. In the first act the king decides to make war on France, having been assured by the clergy that he has a valid claim to the French throne, and by the nobility that there is strong popular support for the proposed and by the nobility that there is strong popular support for the proposed war. The king then receives the French ambassadors, who bring him a case of tennis balls and a contemptuous message from the French dauphin. The reason that the dauphin treats him with such slight regard is that when he was a prince Henry was famous for leading a gay and idle life. We have learned in the first scene, however, from a conversation between the Archbishop of Canterbury and the Bishop of Ely, that Henry has undergone a miraculous transformation since becoming king. Now he has the unqualified respect and admiration of his countrymen. The king sends word to the dauphin that he will answer this mock in the forthcoming war on France.

In the second act all preparations are made for the expedition to France. The king has uncovered a plot against his life, and before the assassins have an opportunity to carry out their plan they are arrested. After hearing Henry's reproaches for their betrayal of king and country, they repent of their treason as they are led off to execution.

In the course of the second act we meet the French king, dauphin, constable, and other high dignitaries. The French appear silly and pompous and they seriously underestimate the threat posed by Henry's invasion. The dauphin is a rash and headstrong young man, who refuses to be convinced that Henry the king is different from Hal the madcap prince. In the third act we see that the English have landed in France and are besieging the town of Harfleur, which finally capitulates when it becomes clear that the reinforcements promised by the dauphin cannot arrive on time. Henry is glad that he does not have to sack the town for both humanitarian and practical reasons. His army is already weakened by disease, and he hopes to march on to the English stronghold of Calais to rest. However, the French, humiliated by the loss of Harfleur, are determined to force an encounter immediately. A French herald asks Henry to surrender voluntarily, since his army is no match for the numerically superior French. Henry refuses. He will neither retreat nor surrender. He will stand where he is and fight if necessary. In the final scene of this act the French nobility are eagerly awaiting the morning and the opportunity of destroying the enemy.

In the fourth act we see that the English soldiers are justly apprehensive on the eve of battle. They know that they are outnumbered by about five to one. Through the long night hours the king goes among his men, trying to cheer them his own confidence in Providence. At one point, disguised by the night and a borrowed cloak, he engages in conversation with three ordinary soldiers. They talk about the duty a subject owes to his sovereign and about the responsibility the king must bear. Henry tells them he thinks the king is a man just as they are. He also says that the monarch cannot be responsible for the souls of his men if they die in battle, as one of the soldiers suggested. At the conclusion of the discussion, an argument arises between Henry and a soldier named Williams. They exchange gloves as tokens by which they can recognize and fight each other after the battle.

Before the battle starts, Henry encourages his men with a rousing speech about the honor they can win this day just because they are so greatly outnumbered. After the fighting begins, it soon becomes apparent that the English are winning a glorious victory. The French acknowledge that they have seriously underestimated their adversary. They surrender, and the casualty list reveals that whereas the French have lost thousands of men, the English have lost very few. Henry gives thanks to God and promises his troops a speedy return to England. In the meantime he has found an opportunity to resolve his quarrel with the soldier (Williams) be revealing his true identity and by rewarding the soldier for his obstinate courage and dignity.

In the fifth act the king and his followers, after some time has elapsed, return to France in order to conclude the peace. Henry woos the French princess in the blunt and good-humored manner of a plain soldier rather than a royal king. The peace terms agreed upon stipulate that Henry shall marry the princess and be accepted as the heir to France upon the death of the present French king. The two warring factions are reconciled and the play ends on a joyous and hopeful note, although the Chorus, in an epilogue, reminds the audience that the English possession of France was lost in the troubled reign of Henry VI.

Simultaneous with the historical action of the play is a comic subplot, involving characters of Shakespeare's imagination. In the second act we meet three rogues preparing to embark with the king's army for France. Bardolph and Pistol are already familiar to audiences of *Henry IV*, but Nym is a new figure in the comedy. They are not at all interested in personal honor or national glory; they are out for loot. Before they can leave, however, Falstaff (the marvelously funny friend of Prince Hal in *Henry IV*) dies, and this briefly dampens their spirits. In France they avoid fighting as much as possible because they are cowardly. Bardolph is hanged for stealing from a church, and Nym also comes to a bad end.

A slightly higher level of comic characters includes the four captains in Henry's army: Gower, Jamy, Macmorris, and especially Fluellen. The latter is a Welshman, very valorous, but very quaint in his ways. He and Pistol quarrel. Pistol threatens to make Fluellen eat his leak (the Welsh national emblem) on Saint Davy's day the Welsh national holiday). Instead, as it turns out in the fifth act, Fluellen forces Pistol to eat the leak. Pistol decides to return to England where he will be a thief, and will doubtless come to a bad end.

# HENRY V

## TEXTUAL ANALYSIS

## ACT 1

### ACT I: SCENE 1

The play opens with a Prologue introducing the action. The Prologue is delivered by the Chorus, who begins by invoking a "Muse of fire."

#### Comment

The Chorus was a common device in the classical drama of ancient Greece and Rome and later in Renaissance drama as well to provide an objective commentary on the action. In early drama the Chorus was composed of many actors speaking in unison. Later their numbers were reduced until finally a single figure represented the point of view of the disinterested spectator. Henry V is the only Shakespearean play to include a Chorus speaking directly to the audience at the beginning of every act.

According to classical mythology these are nine muses, goddesses presiding over the arts. The muse of poetry is often mentioned by ancient poets such as Homer and Vergil, who invoke her aid in their **epic** poems, *The Iliad, The Odyssey,* and *The Aeneid.* These **epic** poems recount the adventures of great heroes such as Odysseus, Achilles, and Aeneas. The first line of *Henry V,* imitating the Greek and Roman fashion of calling upon the muse, is a clue that Shakespeare is writing an **epic** of his own in dramatic form. Like the great ancient epics, *Henry V* portrays a hero king, the model of perfection for a later age. Anxious to do justice to his subject and to overcome the physical limitations of his stage Shakespeare calls upon the spirit of poetry to help him in his task. He calls this spirit a "Muse of fire" because flames naturally tend to rise, and Shakespeare hoped, in *Henry V,* to rise to the heights of imagination and invention.

The Chorus goes on to wish for a stage as large as a kingdom, for princes as actors, and for ruling kings as audience. Only under these conditions will the hero, King Henry, truly appear like a god of war before an audience worthy of him. The Chorus apologizes for daring to tell such a great story with mere actors on a small stage. Comparing the limited area at his disposal with the great expanses of France, he realizes that the entire theater has not room enough to hold even the helmets used in the great battle of Agincourt, which is the **climax** of the play, so this mere play will represent in the imagination the vast areas and mighty personnages of history.

The Chorus asks the spectators to imagine the two great kingdoms of England and France, separated by the narrow English Channel. He asks them to imagine that each man on the stage represents a thousand men and to believe that real horses are visible when horses are talked of by the actors.

The imagination of the audience must clothe the actor for his role and must leap from place to place and from event to event with the story. The Chorus offers to help the audience in this process by commenting on the action. He concludes by requesting patience and a favorable judgment of the play.

## Comment

This is a strange speech for an author to have a character deliver at the beginning of a play. Theatrical performances are by definition representations of events that could not possibly take place on the stage of a playhouse. An audience at a play must "suspend disbelief," that is, must be willing to forget that it is "just a play." When the lights go out, the audience must forget what time of day it is outside and what season of the year it is in real life. Spectators must become unconscious of sitting on chairs in a big auditorium. In short, they must be willing to believe that the men and women on stage are actually living the story that they tell. This is the essence of the theater.

In the prologue of *Henry V,* the Chorus is afraid that the audience will not suspend disbelief in this case. Why is this so? First of all we must remember that Elizabethan theaters did not have stage sets and lighting effects such as modern theaters have. A few simple objects were the only props for the actors. A palace throneroom and a battlefield might be differentiated only by the presence or absence of a few chairs. Therefore, the imagination of the audience had a lot more work to do in Shakespeare's day than in our own. Although Elizabethan actors did use costumes, they were all in contemporary styles. Thus, a king would wear the robes of a sixteenth-century king and a tavernkeeper would wear the outfit of a sixteenth-century hosteler, even if the play was supposed to take place in the early fifteenth century, like *Henry V.*

However, in his other plays Shakespeare did not worry about the audience's failing to suspend disbelief. There are two reasons why he might have been worried in this case. The first reason is that the action takes place in both England and France. Most sixteenth-century history plays did not involve jumps across such great distances (and it is to be remembered that the distance seemed much greater in the sixteenth century than it does in the twentieth). The audience was not accustomed to that particular improbability. The second and more important reason is that Shakespeare was afraid that his hero would not appear heroic enough when played by a mere actor on a paltry stage. If we remember that Shakespeare intended this to be an **epic** drama, we can understand his fear. There are battle scenes in many Shakespearean plays, but only in Henry V does the playwright worry because he cannot have whole armies on stage. Chiefly, he is afraid that anything less than the actual events and characters will diminish their grandeur.

The first scene is a dialogue between two bishops the Archbishop of Canterbury and the Bishop of Ely, at the court of King Henry V of England. They are discussing a bill designed to strip the church of much of its possessions. This bill had come up before the previous king, but had been neither approved nor disapproved because of the continuous civil disorders besetting the government. Canterbury is deeply perturbed by the proposal, which would take from the church all lands bequeathed to it in the wills of devout men. The value of the lands is sufficient to support fifteen earls, fifteen hundred knights, six thousand two hundred squires, and a hundred almshouses caring for the sick and aged, as well as contributing a thousand pounds a year to the a king. This is a great deal of money. The two bishops fear that the church will be left with almost no revenue at all.

## Comment

Henry V came to the throne in 1413 at the death of his father Henry IV. At that time (and, in fact, until the time of Henry VIII in the sixteenth century) England was a Catholic country. The Church was independent of the English government, being ultimately controlled by the pope in Rome, who delegated authority to bishops and priests abroad. The Archbishop of Canterbury was the highest church dignitary in England; the Bishop of Ely was also very important and was probably personal chaplain to the Archbishop. For many years the secular government and the church had been at odds over the question of lands owned by the church. At the time of this play the church owned about half of all English land. Some of this land was used for monasteries, churches and almshouses, but much of it was rented out to feudal lords who provided the church with great sums of money. Many English kings had been anxious to appropriate these churchheld lands for themselves. With estates taken from the church the king could create new lords and squires loyal to himself. With the increased revenues he could afford to equip larger and better armies to fight foreign enemies and to suppress domestic insurrections. Although the bill had not been approved in the time of Henry IV, it was a genuine threat to the church in the still peaceful reign of Henry V.

When Ely asks what can be done to prevent the bill, the Archbishop sidesteps the question and enters into a lengthy speech praising the king. As a prince, he says, Henry (Hal) spent his days among the common people in a life of lighthearted amusements, banqueting and drinking in the taverns and playing at sports. Yet this giddy and self-willed young man underwent an amazing transformation when he ascended the throne. It was as if death had killed his father and his own youthful wildness at one stroke. Canterbury praises King Henry as a "true lover of the holy Church," a scholar, a man with rare ability to argue theology, debate affairs of state, and discuss the complicated art of war. In addition to a keen understanding of many subjects, Henry has the power to charm and to persuade with his sweet and honeyed sentences.

Because as a prince Henry did not spend his time in study and solitude, the Archbishop marvels at his grasp of affairs and his general maturity. Ely replies by comparing Prince Henry to a berry growing beneath a covering of nettles or to summer grass springing up at night unseen. Similarly, the young prince must have been maturing unobserved by those around him.

## Comment

This digression from the subject of the impending bill to the character of the king introduces the **theme** of the play, the greatness of King Henry V. In two earlier plays, *Henry IV,* Part I and *Henry IV,* Part II, Shakespeare had dramatized the story of the extraordinary Prince Hal. In the beginning of Part I, Hal was shown leading a lift of riotous adventures in the company of witty and high-spirited friends. Carousing and playing practical jokes, the prince was the love of the common people but the despair of his father. Compared with another young man named Henry, the valiant and warlike Hotspur, the madcap Prince Hal seemed to his royal father a very disappointing son. The prince was continually in scrapes and rarely presented himself at court. It appeared that he had little interest in affairs of state and even less aptitude for the task of ruling the kingdom.

However, in a famous soliloquy laying bare his innermost thoughts *Henry IV,* Part I, Act I, scene 2), the prince revealed a high degree of self-awareness and purposefulness. Comparing himself to the sun, he declares that he, too, will presently emerge and stun beholders by his glory. Although he enjoyed his wild life while it lasted, he firmly intended to give it up and change his ways when the time came. As in the story of the prodigal son in the New Testament, he knew that there would be more rejoicing over the returning son who had strayed than over the son who had always remained dutifully at home. At the end of *Henry IV,* Part I, when King Henry IV was threatened with an insurrection led by Hotspur, Prince Hal showed the very qualities that his father feared he lacked. Courageous and skillful, he made a gallant show on the battlefield, saving his father's life and killing Hotspur. Moreover, he displayed true nobility of soul by giving Hotspur his just measure of praise and honor, for the prince could appreciate valor even in an enemy. Thus, by the end of *Henry IV,* Part I, Prince Henry showed the makings of a true king and hero.

It was not until *Henry IV,* Part II, however, that he renounced his boisterous companions, particularly Falstaff. This was absolutely necessary when he became king, for he could no longer shut his eyes to disrespect for law and authority. Yet in the course of his friendship with Falstaff and the others, the prince had learned much about the common people and had endeared himself to them. Equally important, with the companions of his youth he had sharpened his wit and imagination, qualities that would help him to be a great king.

The brief discussion of the king's character by the two bishops serves an important function. Before we see and hear King Henry in the next scene, Shakespeare wants us to know something about him. For those in the audience who know their history or are familiar with the two parts of *Henry IV*, the Archbishop's speech serves as a reminder. For those in the audience who do not already know how the background of the play, this quick sketch of character reveals the most important information. When we meet Henry in the following scene we will already know how highly he is respected by his court.

Returning to the subject at hand, Canterbury says that the king has not yet made up his mind about the bill regarding the church lands. In an effort to dissuade him, the Archbishop has urged Henry to press his claim to the French throne by making war on France. By way of encouragement, he has promised the greatest sum of money ever given by the church to a monarch to aid the English effort. The Archbishop did not have time to explain in detail to Henry his legal right to the French crown. Now the French ambassador is about to have an audience with the king, and Canterbury and Ely go off to hear it.

## Comment

The Archbishop is willing to give Henry a great deal of money to prevent his taking over the church lands. He knows that the king will be glad of an opportunity to claim more territory and to follow in the footsteps of his ancestors by making war on France. Therefore he has told the king that he may justly claim the French crown by virtue of his descent from his great-grand-father Edward. The issue of the descent of the crown will be argued in detail in the following scene. In the meantime, it is already clear that Canterbury's chief aim is to preserve the church lands, even if the only way of distracting the king is war against France. The Archbishop is clever and shrewd. We feel that he is more a politician than a spiritual leader.

**SUMMARY**

The Prologue and first scene serve the following purposes:

1. The use of a Chorus and its reference to the muse hint, at the very beginning of the play, that the hero we are about to see will resemble the heroes of the ancient **epics** in nobility and grandeur.

2. The Prologue alerts the audience to the forthcoming jumps in scene between England and France. We are advised that although we will see only a handful of men on one small stage, we must imagine thousands of soldiers on vast fields. Finally, we are warned that the author thinks so highly of his hero that he is afraid no theatrical production can adequately represent him. In other words, our imagination will have to supplement the powers of playwright and actors.

3. The conversation between the two bishops provides the background for the coming events, particularly the war against France. Because they do not want the king to seize church lands, Canterbury and Ely will urge him to claim the French throne and to seek added territory across the water.

4. We are reminded in this scene that as a young man Henry was wild and unreliable, but we are told that now he is a wise and highly respected monarch.

> In the following scene the king will become very angry when the French ambassador refers to his youthful excesses. A knowledge of Henry's early days is essential to an understanding of his character.

## ACT I: SCENE 2

The second scene opens with the entry of the king into a room in the palace, accompanied by several prominent noblemen, Humphrey, Bedford, Clarence, Warwick, Westmoreland, and Exeter. Henry intends to hear the Archbishop before the French ambassador. Canterbury enters and blesses the king, who asks him to explain "justly and religiously" the grounds for his claim to France. Henry emphasizes that he will only press a legitimate and honorable claim and warns the Archbishop against distorting the truth in his interpretation of law and history. The king's advisor will be responsible for every drop of innocent blood shed in a war that results from his faulty counsel.

The Archbishop proceeds to deliver a lengthy and complicated refutation of the French contention that Henry is not the rightful heir to France. The French argument is based on Salique Law, which states that no woman shall succeed her father in Salique land. The French say that the Salique land is France and, therefore, Henry's claim is invalid. However, the Archbishop proves that the Salique land is really a part of Germany. Moreover, he cites historical examples of French kings who came to power on the basis of female rights of succession. Since the French do not apply Salique Law among themselves, they are merely using it as a pretext to keep Henry away.

## Comment

These speeches raise certain problems in the interpretation of Henry's character. He says that he will only fight for a legitimate claim to the throne. That is why it is important that the Archbishop prove that the Salique Law does not apply in France. The question is: does Henry insist on a clarification of the legal issue because deep in his conscience he believes that he must abide by the law of France? Or rather does he insist on legal justification because, as a shrewd politician, he knows how valuable it is to have a basis for his action in law?

Probably Shakespeare intended us to see a combination of both motives in the king. Henry has fought in wars before. He knows that innocent men suffer and die. Surely he has not been untouched by those experiences. On the other hand, he is a king whose life is dominated more by public need than by private scruple. Henry must have learned as a prince that one of the best ways to prevent dissension at home is by waging war abroad. We shall discover in the next act that there are men in England ready to betray the king. A war will distract others so inclined. Moreover, as we shall see later in the scene, the idea of war with France was very popular among the nobles. As a prudent ruler, Henry knows how important it is to consolidate their support.

It may seem to us that Henry is putting an undue amount of responsibility on the Archbishop. After all, it is the king and not any of his advisors who makes the final decision. The real point, however, is political and not moral. Now Henry can say to the world, to his supporters as well as detractors, that he is acting upon the urgent advice of the Archbishop in defense of a clearly proved right.

When Henry again asks if he may "with right and conscience" make this claim, Canterbury assures him that if it is a sin, he will accept full responsibility. Quoting the biblical injunction that the daughter shall inherit from her father, he urges Henry to fight for his right, and to model himself upon his ancestors who led the victorious English in France during the previous century.

Ely, Exeter, and Westmoreland second the arguments of the Archbishop. They remind Henry that he is heir to the blood and courage as well as to the crown of his ancestors. He owes it to them and to himself to make use of his youthful vigor. They declare that the other kings of Europe expect great things of him, that his cause is just, and that no English king ever had richer nobles or more loyal subjects anxious to serve his cause. Finally, Canterbury repeats his promise that the church will raise a greater sum of money than ever before to support the war effort.

## Comment

All the nobles at Henry's court are agreed on one thing: the desirability of war against France. Why should they feel this way? For one thing, they expect to be rewarded with land and money. For another, they probably hope to distinguish themselves in battle. Two other reasons are equally important. The nobility was anxious to reactivate the longstanding feud between England and France in a new campaign. And finally, such a war would be an opportunity to demonstrate the strong sense of personal loyalty that they felt for this particular king, this man, Henry.

The king has one final scruple. He remembers that every time his great grandfather invaded France, the Scots came down upon defenseless England and ravaged the land. This fear is assuaged by Canterbury and Ely, who declare that with careful preparation England can both fight abroad and maintain security at home. Canterbury emphasizes this point in a speech comparing the government of men with that of bees, both of which are based on the principle of obedience. Like men, bees live in a highly organized society ruled by a king (we may wonder why Shakespeare did not know that the chief bee is a queen). Arguing by analogy, the Archbishop declares that just as the bees can coordinate their many different activities, so can men. He suggests that Henry leave three-quarters of his forces at home for the defense of England and take one-quarter with him to fight in France.

The king's mind is made up. Sending for the ambassador, he tells his nobles that with their help and God's he will make France his in fact as it is in right.

## Comment

The Archbishop's description of singing bee-masons building roofs of gold and bee soldiers in "merry march" is charming. However, the real significance of his speech lies rather in his emphasis on obedience as the ruling principle among all living creatures. The Elizabethans tended to seek parallels between the world of nature and the world of man. An argument based on an analogy between bees and humans was likely to be both more familiar and more forceful in the sixteenth century than it is nowadays. In any case, the Archbishop's logic convinces Henry. If unreasoning insects such as bees can do many things at once, surely the English can and will do the same.

In his announcement of his decision to go to war, as in almost every major speech, Henry acknowledges his reliance upon God and his dependence on the nobility. This is significant. Elizabethan England considered the king (and Henry considers himself) to be the agent of God on earth. It is a sign of a king's greatness that while he is proud before men, he is humble before God. Henry never forgets that his success depends ultimately on God and not on himself. His frequent acknowledgment of the nobles is a good political investment. Henry reminds them that he does not underestimate their importance.

At the conclusion of this speech the ambassador of France and his attendants enter. Henry expresses his readiness to know the "pleasure" of the Dauphin (heir apparent of France), who has sent a message. The ambassador begins by asking whether he may speak freely and fully or should merely hint at his meaning. Henry replies with dignity that he is not a tyrant but a "Christian king" who can control his passions. The ambassador may therefore speak without fear.

## Comment

Realizing that he is about to deliver an insult to the king, the ambassador fears the displeasure it will cause. Henry's reply is dignified and regal. The fact that the ambassador asks permission suggests that his experience with the Dauphin has led him to expect lack of self-control in a monarch. Even before the message is delivered, Shakespeare has set up a contrast between the characters of the two opposing princes.

The message from the Dauphin is in reply to Henry's claim to certain dukedoms in France. The French prince taunts the king with references to his youthful wildness, saying that France cannot be won by dances and revels. (The galliard, specifically mentioned by the Archbishop, was a gay dance popular in the sixteenth century. This is one of many **anachronisms** in the play.) Therefore, rejecting the English claim, the Dauphin sends a present, which is revealed to be a barrel of tennis balls.

    Henry cooly thanks the ambassador and says he is glad the Dauphin is "so pleasant with us." Then, waxing impassioned, he declares that when he has tried out these tennis balls in England, he will play a set in France with the French crown at stake. These tennis balls will turn to cannon balls, and France will have cause to weep more than to laugh at the outcome of this jest. The Dauphin does not realize that Henry may be a wiser and a more powerful king because of that very youthful wildness. Henry warns that he is coming on as king of England and of France. And now his object is not only to win his rightful inheritance but to wreak vengeance on the Dauphin for this insult.

## Comment

The game of tennis was known in the sixteenth century as a particularly English game. The Dauphin's jest might have been clever if Henry were a giddy prince interested mainly in sports, although even then it would have been in poor taste. In fact it is not funny at all. Henry has been king for two years at the time this scene takes place. The French prince should have realized by now that Henry the king is very different from what Henry the prince seemed to be. The Dauphin's mock shows lack of judgment as well as scornful rudeness ill becoming a prince. Henry is very proud and he is sensitive about misinterpretations of his past. This insult hurts. But we learn that the king can control his anger and, however, return jest for jest. Punning on several words used in tennis (such as "chace" and "hazard"), he shows that his wit flourishes at moments of tension as well as relaxation. Elizabethan England placed a high value on this kind of verbal agility. Shakespeare would have us admire Henry for his command of language as well as of the sword.

Henry has already decided to make war on France, yet he speaks to the ambassador as if this decision were based on the insulting message from the Dauphin. Why does he do this? The answer is that although we know the truth, the ambassador does not. He will return to France and tell the Dauphin that his impudence is the cause of the war. Henry realizes that it is to his advantage to make the enemy seem to be at fault. It weakens their morale and it makes the English claim seem stronger.

It is interesting to note that in both of Shakespeare's sources Henry decides to go to war after (rather than before) receiving the Dauphin's message. In this play Shakespeare deliberately has this decision precede the ambassador's speech, in order to avoid the suggestion that Henry is acting from a personal motive and in haste. Such an inference would detract from his image as the perfect Christian king.

The Dauphin's message and Henry's reply provide a personal conflict within the larger context of opposing nations. This is dramatically important. An audience is naturally more interested in a struggle between individuals than in a contest between nations. Although we have yet to see and hear the Dauphin in person, we already know that we will not like him. Henry, on the other hand, shows himself worthy of the high praise with which the Archbishop spoke of him in the first scene. His self-control, wit, and eloquence are amply displayed in this speech.

The French ambassador exits with a safe conduct pass from the king, and Exeter remarks ironically that the Dauphin has sent a "merry message." Henry replies that he hopes to make the sender blush for it. Turning to the business at hand, he orders preparations for the war to be completed as quickly as possible.

## Comment

Having made up his mind, the king is all eagerness to proceed with the invasion of France. He is a man of action who does not delay in embarking upon a new project.

### SUMMARY

The second scene of the first act is important for the following reasons:

1. The Archbishop explains why the French are wrong in denying Henry's claim to the French throne. He shows that the Salique Law was never meant for France, and in fact has not been in use there. We can be sure that Henry has every right to wage the war.

2. We learn that Henry is a cautious and a prudent prince. He knows history well enough to remember the danger of a Scottish invasion of England during a war against France. However, he is convinced that the threat is insignificant.

3. We find out that the nobles are strongly in favor of the war. We can be sure that Henry's decision will be popular throughout England, since his subjects believe their king to be a great leader and are willing to give him unqualified support.

4. The Dauphin's insulting message is delivered to the king, whose self-control and politeness are contrasted with the rudeness and poor taste of the French prince. Henry has an opportunity to display his wit and eloquence in his reply to the Dauphin. We see how cleverly the king shifts the responsibility for the war onto the French, even though he has made up his mind before hearing the ambassador.

5. The personal feud between the king and the Dauphin, introduced in this scene, provides a dramatic counterpart to the clash between England and France.

6. By the end of this scene we begin to agree that Henry is worthy to be the hero of an **epic** drama.

# HENRY V

## TEXTUAL ANALYSIS

## ACT 2

### ACT II: SCENE 1

The first scene begins with an introductory speech by the Chorus, describing the changes that have taken place in England since the last act. The whole country, especially the youth, is excited at the prospect of winning honor by following Henry to France. Across the channel, the French tremble at the news of the English preparation. Seeking to avert the invasion, the French resort to conspiracy by bribing three Englishmen to kill the king in Southampton before he sails for France. The three are Richard, Earl of Cambridge; Henry, Lord Scroop of Masham; and Sir Thomas Grey, a knight of Northumberland. At this moment they have been paid, and the king is on his way from London to Southampton, where we will next see him. The Chorus promises the audience a safe and comfortable journey to France in the final scene and an equally easy return to England later in the play. No one will be made seasick by this journey in imagination. The first scene, however, still takes place in London.

## Comment

Once again the Chorus provides us with important information, such as the time and place of the following scenes. In a few brief lines of poetry we are made to feel the fever of excitement and enthusiasm that has swept England since the last act. We also learn of the conspiracy to kill the king, so that we will be able to understand the beginning of the second scene.

The action of the first scene involves the characters of the comic subplot of the play and takes place in London. Bardolph (a lieutenant) and Nym (a corporal) meet on stage and greet each other. We learn that Nym and Ancient Pistol (Ancient was the title of a standard bearer in the army) are no longer friends because Pistol has married Mistress Quickly, the Hostess, to whom Nym had been engaged. The conversation consists mainly of Bardolph's questions and Nym's laconic replies, which reveal his morbid and fatalistic view of the world. Nym is a coward; he tells Bardolph that he doesn't dare to fight Pistol and that he prefers to use his sword for toasting cheese. When Bardolph says he hopes to reconcile Nym and Pistol so that the three of them can go to France together, Nym merely replies that he will live until he dies and do as he may. Things are what they are; knives have edges; and men may be killed when they sleep.

These gloomy generalizations are interrupted by the entrance of Pistol, and the Hostess. Bardolph addresses Pistol as "mine host" (because his wife has kept a tavern), at which Pistol becomes furious (he is given to sudden bursts of anger) and declares that his wife will keep boarders no longer. She agrees to this, affirming that people say she is keeping a brothel merely because fourteen gentlewomen lodge with her. (In Henry IV Mistress Quickly did run a tavern that was also a bawdy house. That is why we must laugh at her remark.)

## Comment

A few general remarks about Shakespeare's use of comedy are in order at this point. Shakespeare realized the value of interspersing comic scenes in the course of the serious action of his plays. This technique, called comic relief, provides a change of mood and of pace in Shakespearean tragedies and histories. It gives the audience a chance to relax and laugh after the heavier scenes. As a rule, the main plot of the history plays concerns people of high rank who speak in **blank verse** (unrhymed iambic **pentameter**). The comic characters, on the other hand, are usually lower class and speak in prose. (We shall note later that one comic character in *Henry V,* Pistol, speaks in blank verse for specifically comic purposes). The main plot (or serious action) and the subplot (or the comic action) are always complementary. That is, each can be understood as a commentary on the other. Thus, in *Henry V* we will have to bear in mind this question: What is the relation between the story of King Henry and the story of Bardolph, Pistol, Nym, and their companions?

All the comic characters in this scene (with the exception of Nym) appeared in either one or both of the two parts of *Henry IV* where, with others, particularly Falstaff, they composed a group of boon companions to Prince Hal. To the Elizabethan audiences, therefore, these characters were already familiar. But, like Henry, they have undergone important changes since the previous plays. In the two parts of *Henry IV,* their rascality was less pronounced than their gaiety, spontaneity, and cleverness. In *Henry V,* however, a certain pall has come over the group. We are made to feel this at the very outset by the gloomy tone of the enigmatic Nym. He at least, we are certain, is not a cheerful fellow of the sort that appears in *Henry IV.* The quarrel between Pistol and Nys is another sign that things are not quite the same among this group of friends.

Suddenly the Hostess notices Nym, and he and Pistol draw swords. Bardolph intervenes, thinking to stop them, but this is unnecessary; the two prefer name-calling to fighting. Pistol calls Nym an "Iceland dog" and a "viper vile." When the corporal tells the Hostess that he wants her "souls" (meaning both alone and unmarried), Pistol delivers some flashing verbal retorts but still does nothing. Bardolph again bids them put up their swords and they comply, but Pistol still cannot control his tongue and renews his insults. He is interrupted by the arrival of the Boy, who asks them to come to his master, Falstaff, who is lying very ill upstairs. The Hostess goes off, declaring that the king has surely killed poor Falstaff's heart.

Bardolph again tries to reconcile Nym and Pistol, who now quarrel over eight shillings that Nym won from Pistol in a bet. Pistol refuses to pay, "Base is the slave that pays:" Nym insists and again they draw swords. At this point Bardolph intervenes with an oath and the two quarrelers come to terms. Pistol will give Nym a noble (a coin worth about six shillings), liquor, and his friendship. This friendship is worth something, for Pistol has been appointed provisioner to the army and offers to share with his companions the benefits of this profitable position. On this basis Nym agrees and peace is restored.

Now the Hostess rushes in, begging them to come to Falstaff, who is dying upstairs. All grieve that the king has broken poor Falstaff's heart but Pistol complacently remarks that though Falstaff die, "we will live.

### Comment

The belligerence of both Nym and Pistol is a sham. Both men are cowards, neither wants to fight, and the contras between their words and their deeds constitutes much of the humor of this scene. Equally comic are Pistol's speeches. This wrathful individual has a knack for making up outrageous epithets, which he delivers in the sonorous **blank verse** that Shakespeare usually reserved for his serious characters. All the others in this scene speak in prose. The contrast between the style and content of Pistol' speeches is extremely funny. The Boy's entry puts a stop to the comedy just when it has reached its height. News of Falstaff's critical condition does not lend itself to humor.

The reconciliation of the two antagonists is based on the profit motive. Bardolph, Pistol, and Nym agree to go to France together in order to make the most of their connection with the army. In the context of this fiercely patriotic play, their selfish greed is particularly odious. Bawdiness and pompousness can make us laugh, but contempt for the honor and welfare of England is not amusing.

Sir John Falstaff is probably the wittiest man in English literature. He figures in four of Shakespeare's plays: *Henry IV* Part I and Part II, *Henry V,* and *The Merry Wives of Windsor.* The last was written at the specific request of Queen Elizabeth, who wanted to see more of that funny man Falstaff. In *Henry IV* Part I he is the prince's dearest friend and, we feel, justly so. A fat man past middle age, Falstaff has an enormous capacity for food, drink, women, and wit, and none at all for conventional morality. He has no use for concepts such as honor and respect for authority. In *Henry IV* Part II, when the prince became king, he turned his back on Falstaff and his way of life. In the very last scene of the play the new king told his former friend in no uncertain terms, "I know thee not, old man; fall to thy prayers," and banished him from the royal presence on pain of death. Now in *Henry V* we are told that the king has broken the old man's heart. Nym is remarkably perceptive when he observes in his usual laconic style that, "The king is a good king, but it must be as it may." In truth, Henry is a good king, but being a good king often means not being a loyal friend. Henry's unkindness to Falstaff is an example of the hurt a man sometimes inflicts on a close friend for the sake of the high political office he holds. In the next scene we will see an example of a hurt a king may sometimes have to suffer for the same reason.

### SUMMARY

This scene is important for the following reasons:

1. It introduces us to some of the characters who will provide comic relief throughout the play. Many of them are familiar from *Henry IV* Part I and Part II, but in this scene we learn that they are not quite the same as they use to be. Nevertheless, they are still very amusing, particularly loud-mouthed Pistol and glum, laconic Nym, who is new in *Henry V* and reappears in *The Merry Wives of Windsor.*

2. We learn that Falstaff is very sick and likely to die. The Hostess blames the king for breaking the old man's heart.

3. Bardolph, Nym, and Pistol are planning to join the king's army in France. We may expect to find them there later in the play.

## ACT II: SCENE 2

The second scene takes place in Southampton, where the king and army are ready to embark for France. Bedford, Exeter, and

Westmoreland enter, discussing the conspiracy against the king's life, which Henry has discovered. They marvel at the traitors' powers to dissemble, and they are amazed at the participation in the plot of one man particularly dear to the king.

Henry comes on stage accompanied by various lords, including the three conspirators, Scroop, Cambridge, and Grey, who do not yet know that they have been found out. They assure Henry that no king was ever better loved or more feared than he. Grey says that even those who were his father's enemies have been won over to his side. Henry replies that he is completely confident of the loyalty of all his subjects, both those who will accompany him to France and those who will remain in England. Turning to Exeter, Henry bids him set free a man recently imprisoned for speaking ill of the king while drunk. All three conspirators protest against this leniency, urging Henry to make this man an example for others. When the king says, "O, let us yet be merciful," they declare that allowing such a man to live after severe punishment is mercy enough. But Henry is determined to free the prisoner. If slight misdeeds committed under the influence of wine are not forgiven, how shall we react to more serious crimes, he asks. Then, turning to his three false friends, he hands each one a paper which he says is his commission for the army, but is really a warrant for arrest. Reading the papers, the three grow pale, confess their fault, and throw themselves upon the mercy of the king.

Comment

Bedford, Westmoreland, and Exeter precede the others on stage to remind us what we were told by the Chorus in the first scene, that a conspiracy against the king's life has been discovered, although the traitors have not yet been arrested.

After the king and others enter, the arrest does not take place immediately. We are given an opportunity to observe how Scroop, Cambridge, and Grey play the part of loyal and devoted subjects. We contrast their hardheartedness with the generosity of the king, who can forgive a minor offense. The conspirators probably think that they can best show love for Henry by demanding severe punishment for the man who maligned him. In fact, however, both we and the king know of their treachery and we realize that Henry is making them speak the words with which he will presently condemn them. **Irony** abounds in the exchanges between Henry and his would-be assassins. When he assures them of his confidence in the loyalty of all his subjects, we know that he knows of their plot. They, however, take his words as proof of his ignorance of their conspiracy. Again, when he says that they will discover in their commissions how truly he knows their "worthiness," we are aware that Henry knows what they are up to. They, on the other hand, know nothing of the sort. This scene has great dramatic impact. Because we understand the king better than the conspirators do, we can appreciate the **irony** of his words. As the scene proceeds, the tension grows, until the conspirators discover that they have been caught.

The king delivers a long speech, reproaching his former friends for planning to commit treason and murder. How do they dare, for very shame, to ask for mercy! They themselves have just warned Henry against showing clemency to a man who merely attacked the king with words. They would have taken his life. By their own advice, then, he ought not to show mercy and he will not do so.

What makes their plotting most cruel is that Henry has loved and trusted these men, particularly Scroop, whom he now calls an "Ingrateful, savage, and inhuman creature." Henry cherished, trusted, and confided in this man above others. Scroop ought to have been the last man in England to turn traitor, for he seemed serious, scholarly, and religious, moderate in his passions and prudent in his judgment. In the light of what Scroop seemed to be, his fall seems to Henry like another fall of man. Henceforth the king will suspect even the most virtuous men of secret duplicity. Ordering the arrest of the traitors, he commits them to the mercy of God.

## Comment

*Henry V* is not only about the triumphs of a great king; it is also about the personal sacrifices demanded by high office. In this scene we witness a specific example of the general truth that all men in high position are threatened by betrayal. Henry's speech is a moving account of the love and admiration he felt for his friend Scroop. He is grieved and shocked to discover evil in a man he thought so near perfection. His language is unusually strong, for his emotion is strongly roused.

In the first act we learned that Henry is particularly well suited for the difficult office of the king. He is regal without being haughty; proud yet self-controlled; eager to claim his right, but always prudent where the security of England is concerned. We know that Henry is a man who rules his personal life in accordance with the demands of his public image. Thus, as soon as his friendship with Falstaff became a political liability he put an end to it. We are never made to feel that the king has any regrets at sacrificing his friendship to political expediency. Scroop's betrayal, on the other hand, causes the king noticeable anguish. There is a curious parallel between Henry's abandoning Falstaff and Scroop's betraying Henry, neither of which would have occurred had Henry not been king. If he had been an ordinary man, he could have continued to enjoy

Falstaff's company; and no one would have thought to bribe Scroop to betray him. Therefore we see that both these personal losses are contingent upon Henry's being king of England. In regard to Falstaff, Henry was the agent (consciously acting in accordance with the best interests of the kingship), whereas in regard to Scroop Henry is the victim. A king always has enemies who will try to corrupt his closest friends; they are bound to succeed at times. As a result of this betrayal the king's faith in human loyalty is shaken. From now on he will be a less trusting and therefore an even lonelier man.

Exeter pronounces each man under arrest and, one by one, Scroop, Cambridge, and Grey express their repentance. Scroop declares that God has justly revealed their evil purpose and begs Henry to forgive his fault but not his body. The two others share his feelings.

In pronouncing sentence, the king declares that he seeks no personal revenge. As guardian of the country, however, he must sentence to death men who would have subjected lords and commons alike to foreign oppression and contempt. He hopes that God in His mercy will give the traitors true repentance and endurance to bear their death.

## Comment

The repentance of the conspirators is one of the weaker moments in the play. Undoubtedly Shakespeare did not want to mar the unblemished portrait of the king with the persistent opposition of three important Englishmen. Their change of heart makes unanimous the English devotion to Henry. Yet we may well ask ourselves what motivated these three men to treason in the first place. If they admire the king after he has sentenced them to death, why were they disloyal while they enjoyed his favor? Cambridge says that the French gold was not his real reason, though he does not tell us what was. As for Grey and Scroop, we can only believe that in their cupidity they succumbed to French bribery. Yet this is hard to understand, since Henry is a generous king and has not failed to reward them in the past. We may wonder to ourselves if perhaps these men were not actually critical of Henry in ways which Shakespeare does not choose to mention, for to do so would undercut his description of the hero-king.

Henry is not by nature a man to bear grudges. We feel that this is so when he sets free the prisoner who had made seditious remarks about him. Toward the traitors he is neither malicious nor cruel. He expresses only sorrow at their betrayal, not hatred of them. If the demands of the kingship conflict with his personal inclination toward mercy, he will act in accordance with his duty. The death sentence is public justice, not private revenge.

As the three traitors are taken off-stage by guards. Henry turns his attention to the expedition against France. He interprets the discovery of the plot as a sign of God's favor. With no other hindrance, they may commit themselves to the hands of God and put to sea. Henry will be "No king of England if not king of France."

### Comment

There remains no further obstacle to the expedition. We may therefore expect to see the king next in France, as we shall in the third act.

## SUMMARY

This scene is important for the following reasons:

1. We are allowed to observe the three conspirators and to notice how they pretend a loyalty they do not feel. Henry's predisposition toward mercy is in marked contrast to their hardheartedness.

2. The conversation between the king and his "friends" is highly ironical. Henry knows, and we know, that his words often have a hidden meaning that the conspirators fail to grasp. This **irony** heightens the tension of the scene.

3. Henry's denunciatory speech reveals that, after all, he is a man who, like other men, can be deeply hurt by the cruel desertion of a friend. We learn that he greatly loved and admired Scroop and that he will never again be so trusting in friendship.

4. The conspirators repent of their treachery and rejoice in the prevention of their crime. Thus we see that all of England is now unanimous in support of Henry. However, the character and motivation of the conspirators remain unclear.

5. Henry sentences the traitors to death as he must do. He is not a man to be swayed by hatred or the desire for revenge. As he said of himself in the second scene of the first act, he is a "Christian king."

6. We learn that the army is now ready to set sail for France.

## ACT II: SCENE 3

Pistol, Bardolph, and Nym are leaving London for Southampton to embark with the army. The Hostess asks her husband if she may go part of the way with them, but he says no, for he is still grieving over the death of Falstaff (which has taken place since the first scene of this act). The conversation then turns to the subject of Falstaff's death. Bardolph wishes he were with him in heaven or in hell. The Hostess quickly replies that Falstaff is in heaven, for his death was as peaceful as any innocent child's. She relates how she could tell he was dying by the way he fumbled with the sheets, and toyed with flowers, and smiled at his fingers. His nose looked sharp and pinched and he babbled about green fields. At one point he cried out "God, God, God" until she tried to comfort him by saying that there was no need yet to think of God. But his body was cold as a stone, and he died.

Nym says that Falstaff cried out a warning against sack (the Rhine wine he had loved to drink), and Bardolph adds that he also cried out a warning against women. This second point the Hostess tries to deny, although she admits that it may be so, for he talked of the Whore of Babylon. (The Hostess, who kept a brothel herself, does not want to think that the devil will have Falstaff on account of women. In that case she would be partly responsible. The Whore of Babylon is a religious reference, which the Hostess and the others probably do not understand, although the audience should. In the Book of Revelation in the New Testament the Whore of Babylon stands for the antichrist.) The Boy remembers how Falstaff thought a fly on Bardolph's nose was a soul burning in hell. Bardolph (who is known for having a fiery red nose) says that "the fuel is gone that maintained that fire" (meaning that Falstaff is dead, for Bardolph was in his employ and got the money to pay for his wine and therefore his red nose indirectly from Falstaff).

The men prepare to leave. Pistol bids farewell to his wife, kissing her and telling her to guard his property, to give no credit to customers, to trust no one, and to be cautious in all things. They are off to France, he says, to suck like leeches the enemy's very blood (which the Boy remarks is a very unwholesome food). They exit.

## Comment

We have already remarked that the comic characters in *Henry V* are far less delightful than those in *Henry IV,* and this is chiefly due to the absence of Falstaff, who always manages to charm us no matter what he does. In *Henry IV* Falstaff drank and cahoused outrageously, yet neither he nor the audience felt that his activities were sins. We admired his zest for life, his spontaneity, and ingenuity. In *Henry V,* however, we are told that Falstaff died in a religious frame of mind, warning against drink and fearing that the devil would get him on account of women.

What was Shakespeare's intention when he described the dying Falstaff as a changed man? First we must remember that in *Henry V* Falstaff is old and sick, and that many people who are irreligious in their prime begin, as they near death, to believe that perhaps the church is right after all and to fear the punishment of hell.

This is the realistic explanation of the manner of Falstaff's death. But there is another explanation as well. Falstaff's delightful defiance of conventional morality and decorum is incompatible with the austere dignity of King Henry. We cannot simultaneously be charmed by Falstaff's irregular behavior and impressed by Henry's regal self-command. Therefore it is necessary for the consistency of our vision that Falstaff die with a changed attitude, repenting of his "sins" as Henry had bid him do at the end of *Henry IV* Part II ("I know thee not, old man; fall to thy prayers"). The description of Falstaff's death superimposes a genuine pathos on hilarious comedy.

In the second part of the scene we learn something of Pistol's vision of the world. He warns his wife not to trust anyone, for he himself is not to be trusted and he generalizes from himself to all mankind. His purpose in going to France is not to fight an honorable war, but to "suck the blood," that is, to gain what he can in the way of plunder and loot. His image of himself, Bardolph, and Nym as leeches is really very apt. Indeed, we think of them as low creatures who prey on others. Although his pompous language is absurdly funny, we sense that Pistol and his companions are essentially contemptible.

**SUMMARY**

This scene is a short interlude in the serious action of the play. It serves to describe Falstaff's death and to see Bardolph, Pistol, and Nym off for France, where we shall meet them.

## ACT II: SCENE 4

The scene now shifts to France, where the French king is discussing the threatening state of affairs with his chief advisors, the dukes of Berri and Britaine, the Constable of France, and the Dauphin. Concerned about the condition of the French defenses, the king asks the four dukes and the Dauphin to mobilize the men and supplies necessary to fortify the towns along the path of the approaching English. The Dauphin replies that although a nation should at all times be in a state of preparedness, there is no present cause to fear England, for her king is "a vain, giddy, shallow, humorous youth." The Constable objects to this evaluation of Henry and bids the Dauphin heed the reports of the French ambassadors who have just returned from England. These ambassadors have great respect for the English king, and particularly for the calm determination with which he is pursuing his present course of action. The Constable compares Henry to the Roman Brutus (Lucius Junius Brutus pretended to be stupid in order to avoid suspicion while plotting against Tarquin, the king) and to a rose bush that is covered with manure before it yields the sweetest flowers.

The Dauphin is unimpressed by these arguments, but he grants that it is wiser to overestimate than underestimate the power of the enemy. His father, however, thinks King Henry strong, and not only because of what the ambassadors report. The French king remembers Edward the Black Prince, who led the victorious English in the battle of Crecy, and he fears that Henry has inherited the prowess and courage of his warlike ancestor.

### Comment

In this scene we meet the major figures on the French side, who are contrasted with the English. The French king is much older than Henry of England. He is genuinely concerned about the danger threatening his country and his crown. He has learned from experience and from history that the English are to be feared, not treated with contempt. The Dauphin, on the other hand, seems to be a rash young man who sticks to his own opinions about Henry (whom he has never met) in spite of what better informed sources say. Others in the French court, particularly the Constable, have altered their estimation of the

English king. The Constable of France was the commander-in chief of the French army in the absence of the monarch and therefore a very important person. Here the obstinacy of the Dauphin is contrasted with the greater mental flexibility of the Constable.

At this point a messenger announces the arrival of an ambassador from Henry. The king remarks that the English are advancing quickly. Urging his father not to show weakness, the Dauphin compares the English to "coward dogs," who yell loudly when their prey runs away, but who dare not stand and fight.

Exeter enters accompanied by attendants. His message from Henry to the king is a demand for the crown of France, which he claims by right of his descent from Edward the Third. The laws of God, of nature, and of nations confirm this right. If France will not yield peacefully, Henry intends to compel assent by force of arms. "Therefore in fierce tempest is he coming." He bids the French king resign the crown and spare the widows, orphans, and bereaved sweethearts who will otherwise mourn for husbands, fathers, and lovers slain in battle. This is Henry's message to the king. He has sent another for the Dauphin.

The French king promises to consider his answer carefully and to have it ready by the following day. Then the Dauphin asks for his message from England, and Exeter conveys Henry's scorn, defiance, contempt, and everything in the way of slight regard that is not unbecoming a prince to express. If the Dauphin's father does not grant the English demands, a fierce and bloody war will answer the mock the French prince sent. To this the Dauphin replies that nothing will please him more than war with England, and that he sent the tennis balls on purpose to engender animosity. Exeter warns that the French will learn to their sorrow that Henry is a far different man as king than he seemed to be as prince. He announces that the English have already landed in France and urges the French king to prepare an answer as quickly as possible.

## Comment

We learned in this first act that Henry's original demand for the crown of France was scornfully rejected. There is little reason to hope that the French will accede peacefully to his demands now, since they consider their forces to be at least the equal of the English. Exeter's message, therefore, is really more of a formal announcement of the English arrival on French soil than a serious expectation that the French will yield. Henry's final attempt to avoid war by appealing to the French king's compassion for his people may call to mind the two other occasions on which he reminded others of the suffering that inevitably accompanies war. The first was in his speech to the Archbishop and the second in his reply to the Dauphin's gift of the tennis balls, both in Act I, Scene 2. In all three cases Henry reveals his keen awareness of the terrible human tragedies that take place in wartime and his desire to avert them if possible, that is, without sacrificing his honorable cause. We will discuss this issue in greater detail when it is raised again in Act III, Scene 3 and in Act IV, Scenes 1 and 7. Henry's reply to the Dauphin emphasizes the difference between the two young men. The English king, always conscious of his regal position, is careful to send such messages of scorn as do not detract from his own dignity. By implication we may conclude that he judges the Dauphin's mock to be the kind of message unbecoming a prince. Exeter confirms what the French ambassadors have already reported, namely, that the king is a most impressive monarch. The French court can now have little doubt as to the true nature of their opponent.

## SUMMARY

This scene is important for the following reasons:

1. We are introduced to the French king and lords, among whom the Dauphin and the Constable are most prominent. We shall have occasion to see them again. In the meantime we learn that the king is concerned over the welfare of his kingdom and is preparing to strengthen the French defenses. The Dauphin obstinately persists in his low opinion of King Henry and his contempt for the English in general. The French king and the Constable, more mature in their judgment, realize that there is good reason to think Henry strong. We are again reminded of Henry's fearful ancestor, Edward, the Black Prince of Wales.

2. We learn that the English have already landed in France and we will be prepared to see them in the next act besieging the town of Harfleur.

3. Exeter's message gives the French king one last chance to surrender peacefully. We are reminded of Henry's awareness that war always makes new widows and orphans.

4. Henry's regal message to the Dauphin is contrasted with the trifling mock he received from that prince.

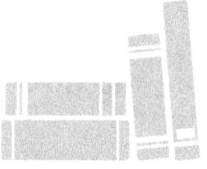

# HENRY V

## TEXTUAL ANALYSIS

## ACT 3

### ACT III: SCENE 1

The Chorus introduces this act as he introduces the others, by describing the events that have intervened between the last act and the following scene. We must imagine that we have seen the king's majestic fleet embark at Southampton. He bids us see in our mind's eye silken streamers flying from the masts and shipboys climbing on the rigging. In our mind's ear we must hear the shrill sound of the ship's whistle, issuing commands to the crew as the invisible wind draws "the huge bottoms through the furrowed sea." The Chorus bids us imagine that we are on the shore and watching a veritable city dancing on the waves, for this royal armada is like nothing so much as a city afloat on the water.

As the king holds his course for the French port of Harfleur, we shall follow him, leaving behind a silent England guarded only by grandfathers and infants. Every Englishman of strength and honor is determined to prove his manhood by the side of the king and his noblemen in France. Now we must imagine the English arrived at Harfleur, their cannon trained on the town. Exeter returns to Henry from the French court with an offer of Katherine, the French princes, in marriage together with several minor dukedoms. These peace terms are unacceptable. The English cannons open fire on Harfleur.

Comment

The vivid poetry of the Chorus makes a gay picture of the English fleet sailing across the Channel. When he talks of "huge bottoms" (bottoms is the technical word for ships, and not just a reference to the bottom of the vessel) drawn through the "furrowed sea," we must remember that even though the English Channel is a relatively narrow body of water, it is known for being particularly rough and tempestuous. Nowadays, a Channel crossing is a minor affair, but in the fifteenth century it was much more of an expedition. Although the English had long been active mariners, it was not until the reign of Queen Elizabeth, and the defeat of the Spanish Armada in 1588 that England became mistress of the seas. The vision of a majestical fleet dancing like a city on the waves was undoubtedly relished by a nation proud of its great sea power.

We may remember that in the second scene of the first act, when Henry was weighing the dangers of an invasion of France, he recalled the possibility of Scottish descent upon a defenseless England. For this reason the Archbishop advised the king to take only a quarter of his army with him and to leave the rest behind. Now, however, the Chorus tells us that only infants and old men remain to protect England. Why the discrepancy? History tells that Henry did, in fact, leave a sufficient defense behind. Therefore we must conclude that the Chorus's speech is intended to emphasize the popular enthusiasm for the war by exaggerating the truth. In the last scene of the second act the French king was considering what answer to send Henry. Now we learn what that answer was. One very common way of establishing good relations between opposing monarchies was by a marriage uniting the two royal houses. The closeness between man and wife, it was hoped, would result in closeness between the two nations. Moreover, a bride was always given a dowry, that is, a certain amount of property and money that she brought to her husband. In the case of royal marriages, this led to the consolidation of larger and larger states. All modern European nations were formed from petty dukedoms welded together by war and marriage. *Henry V* used both methods. At the end of this play we shall see him marry the same Princess Katherine whom he now rejects. The minor dukedoms that were first offered as her dowry were insufficient for an English king laying claim to all of France.

The Chorus concludes by preparing us to see the siege of Harfleur in the next scene. We shall have to imagine battle conditions only suggested on stage.

The action of the first scene is very brief. It takes place during the siege of Harfleur and consists entirely of Henry's speech rallying his men: "Once more into the breach, dear friends, once more, / Or close the wall up with our English dead." (Medieval towns were surrounded by walls for protection. An attacking army therefore had to lay siege to the town either by scaling the walls or by making an entry way with their cannons. Such an entry point was called the breach and there the fighting was fierce.) Henry urges his men forward again, bidding them imitate the ferocity of the tiger. The gentle qualities that become a man in peacetime should be exchanged in time of war for savagery and violence. Instead of looking calm and mild, the warrior must assume a terrifying appearance to suit the fierceness of his actions.

## Comment

Henry is a master at generating enthusiasm among his men both by the example of his deeds and the power of his oratory. His comparison of the soldier and the tiger shows a keen observation of nature, for men really do bare their teeth, stretch their nostrils wide, and tense their muscles in combat just as animals do. Like animals, men are unconscious of these changes in appearance, and Henry does not mean that they should now deliberately assume such expressions. Rather he intends to stir their imagination and arouse their fervor. We will have occasion to recall these remarks when we come to Henry's long speech in the third scene of this act.

Continuing his oration, the king reminds the lords of their noble ancestors and bids them not dishonor their fathers and mothers in this encounter. He tells them to be models to the other soldiers ("men of grosser blood") and teach them how to war. Then, turning to the yeomen (farmers), he urges them to prove the quality of their rearing, for no one on this battlefield, however low his rank, lacks a "noble lustre" in his eyes. Comparing his army to greyhounds straining at the leash before the hunt, he declares, "The game's afoot!" and orders the charge with the cry "God for Harry! England and Saint George!"

## Comment

Henry's army is composed of nobles and yeomen, and he addresses particular remarks to each group. His words to the lords appeal to their sense of honor and tradition as incentives for the present day. The idea of "blood" was very important in feudal society, which believed that nobility was carried through the blood literally as well as figuratively. No member of the aristocracy could remain indifferent to the honor of the bloodline from which he was descended and which his children would carry on. In feudal society the nobility constituted the warrior class. That is, the landed gentry were responsible for providing and leading their own men in support of the king. Moreover, according to the feudal system of hierarchies, the vassal looked to his suzerain for spiritual as well as material superiority. Thus, Henry always tries to set the best possible example for his vassals (the nobility) and they, in turn, must set the standard for the yeomen.

Turning to the yeomen, Henry couches his appeal in terms of the honor of their land. The concept of blood honor does not apply to them. In the context of twentieth-century democracy we might find this distinction in rank unpleasant, but it was in accordance with established social patterns of fifteenth - and sixteenth-century England and therefore would not have given offense. We should think of it as if a modern general were to address himself first to his officers, then to the common soldiers, and finally to both. As a matter of fact, we may note here that the yeomen were the most effective component of the English army, during the Hundred Years' War. Their use of the longbow gave the English a decisive advantage over the French, who depended primarily upon a shorter bow and heavily armored cavalry.

There is great gaiety in Henry's concluding words as he compares the war not to a bloody and fearful encounter but to a game. In this way he makes it seem both easy and merry. His motto, delivered in a ringing cry, calls upon the king by his more familiar name, Harry, rather than the more formal Henry, and reminds his listeners that God is for Harry and Harry's war. Saint George, the patron saint of England, was famous for slaying dragons. As the scene ends with this ringing cry, we feel certain that the war will be a glorious triumph.

**SUMMARY**

In this scene the following important developments take place:

1. The Chorus carries us in imagination across the English Channel to France together with Henry's army. We learn that the French king has offered unsatisfactory peace terms and, therefore, that Henry will proceed to besiege Harfleur. The French princess Katherine is mentioned for the first time here. We will meet her later in the play.

2. Henry's speech to his men during the siege demonstrates his abilities as a leader. He appeals to the different classes among his followers in terms that they will understand and appreciate. His oratory is dramatic and charged with emotion. Although there are only a few men on stage, we are made to feel that we are in the midst of a real battle.

## ACT III: SCENE 2

Bardolph, Pistol, Nym, and the Boy pause to rest during the siege. Bardolph urges the others back to the fighting, but they know him well enough to realize that he is as content as they are to remain safely away from the fray. Nym remarks that he has only one life, and the battlefield is no place to preserve it.

Pistol agrees, and breaks into a little song telling how immortal fame is won on the battlefield. The Boy says he does not care about fame. He wishes he were safe in a London alehouse and he joins in Pistol's song. At this light-hearted moment, Captain Fluellen enters and orders the shirkers back to the breach. They go off, but only after Pistol begs Fluellen in absurdly comic terms to "abate thy rage." Left alone on the stage, the Boy reveals in a soliloquy what he knows of the other three. Although he is their servant and younger then they, he is more honorable than three such buffoons put together. Bardolph, he says, is white-livered (cowardly) and red-faced; therefore he never fights. Pistol's words are fierce enough to kill, if words could kill, but his sword hurts no one. Therefore he breaks his word (because he never performs the deeds he promises) and keeps his sword intact. Nym, on the other hand, is a man of few words, but the few he does say are as bad as most of his actions. These three rascals will steal anything. Bardolph, for example, stole the case of a lute (a popular stringed instrument resembling a guitar), carried it a great distance, only to sell it for a few pennies. They want the Boy to steal also, but this villainy goes against his nature, and he determines to seek some other service.

## Comment

Bardolph's words upon entering, are a direct **parody** of the first line of Henry's speech in the preceding scene. "On, on on, on, on! to the breach, to the breach!" says Bardolph, where the king had cried "Once more unto the breach, dear friends, once more." But whereas the king had fervently appealed to his soldiers in terms of honor and duty. Bardolph, like his companions, is anxious only to save his own life. They agree with Falstaff in *Henry IV Part I* (Act V, Scene 4) that "The better part of valor is discretion," for honor means nothing to them. In this play, where courage and fame are glorified, their cowardice is more despicable than amusing. Captain Fluellen is also a comic character, as we shall soon, see, but he is in dead earnest about the war.

The Boy's soliloquy tells us what we already know about the character of his companions, but we learn that he is different from them, for he is no thief. A soliloquy is a speech delivered by a character alone on the stage and is used to reveal his inner thoughts. Shakespeare usually reserved soliloquies for major characters of the main plot. The only other soliloquy in this play is spoken by Henry in the fourth act. Here, the Boy's inner thoughts accord with our own, and with the values of King Henry, and they are therefore suitable material for such a speech.

Captains Fluellen and Gower enter separately and Gower summons Fluellen to come to the Duke of Gloucester at the mines. Fluellen declares that the mines are no good, that they are not deep enough. Gower maintains that Macmorris, chief advisor to the Duke of Gloucester who is in charge of the siege, is a valiant Irishman. Fluellen disagrees. He believes that anyone who does not know or care about Roman military science must be a fool, and the Irishman is such a one.

At this point Macmorris himself comes in with Captain Jamy, a Scotsman whom Fluellen praises for his valor and for his knowledge of the ancient wars. Macmorris begins to lament that his mines have not been used to blow up the walls of the town as they could have done. Fluellen, preoccupied with his one overriding interest, asks Macmorris to enter into a discussion of the Roman wars. Captain Jamy appears to share Fluellen's interest, but Macmorris does not. The middle of a siege is no time for discourse, he declares, especially with the trumpet summoning them to the breach. "Tis shame for us all," he asserts, to be standing here when "there is throats to be cut, and works to be done." Captain Jamy is torn, for he would have liked to hear the debate; but he swears that before the day is over he will do good service or lie dead on the ground. Fluellen, however, is not yet ready to abandon his argument with Macmorris and, therefore, with excessive politeness, refers to the Irishman's "nation." A regular quarrel is brewing, when the trumpet sounds a parley (for talks between the opposing sides), thereby putting a stop to the controversy although Fluellen manages to get in a last word about the "disciplines of war."

## Comment

Fluellen, Gower, Macmorris, and Jamy are comic characters but a very different sort from Pistol, Bardolph, and Nym. These captains take the science of warfare in general and this war in particular very seriously. Though they disagree among themselves, they all take great pride in their role as soldiers. When they clash, it is largely a matter of temperament and of chauvinistic pride. Fluellen is pedantic, obstinate, proud, and blunt. He is probably jealous of Macmorris for being chief advisor to the Duke of Gloucester. Later we will see other instances of Fluellen's readiness to pick a quarrel, whether on his own behalf or that of the king. In these scenes we learn of his overwhelming interest in and respect for the science of warfare as practiced by the Romans. He is the sort of man who feels that no one can be worth very much who does not share his personal enthusiasms. Of the four men, Fluellen has the greatest significance in this play.

Another important aspect of this scene is the national background of the four captains. Fluellen is Welsh, Gower English, Macmorris Irish, and Jamy is Scots, as we can tell from their names as well as their pronunciation. Fluellen pronounces his "b's" as "p's;" Macmorris says "ish" for "is," "Chrish" for "Christ," and Jamy says "theise" for "these" and "gud" for "good." Thus we have a quick sampling of the pronunciations common in the different parts of Britain in Shakespeare's time.

It is important to note that although these captains may quarrel among themselves on minor matters, they are unanimous in their support of the king. Macmorris therefore becomes highly indignant when Fluellen refers to his "nation" as if to impugn his loyalty. This national solidarity is a great triumph for Henry. For many years before and after his reign, English kings had serious difficulties with rebellions among the Welsh, the Irish, and the Scots. We may recall that Henry IV was constantly troubled with uprisings in the north, and that Henry V expressed doubts about the loyalty of the Scots in the first act. At the time this play was written, the Irish were in rebellion against Queen Elizabeth, and a reference is made to this fact in the Chorus' introduction to the fifth act. The participation of these four captains suggests that Henry has been able to win the allegiance of the frequently rebellious areas of his kingdom.

**SUMMARY**

The significance of this scene is that:

1. We have greater reason to feel contempt for Pistol, Bardolph, and Nym than we did before we witnessed their cowardice and heard the Boy's speech describing their thieving ways. If Henry's oratory of the previous scene cannot arouse their sense of honor nothing can.

2. We are introduced to Fluellen, Gower, Macmorris, and Jamy, who symbolize Henry's firm supporters among the Welsh, Irish, and Scots.

3. Some of Fluellen's peculiarities become apparent. We shall see these oddities, as well as others, later in the play.

4. We learn that a parley has been sounded, and may therefore expect to hear a conversation between Henry and the governor of Harfleur in the following scene.

## ACT III: SCENE 3

Speaking to the governor of Harfleur, who is standing upon the walls of the city, Henry offers the French one last chance to surrender. If they refuse, the king declares upon his honor as a soldier that he will not cease the onslaught until the city lies buried in her ashes. As yet, Henry can still restrain his men, but he warns that if the battery is resumed and the city taken, he will be as powerless to control them as to command a leviathan (a mythical sea monster). He prophesies destruction, pillage, and slaughter if the fighting begins again. The common soldier, he warns, "In liberty of bloody hand shall range / With conscience wide as hell, mowing like grass / Your fresh fair virgins and your flowering infants." Mercy will then be out of the question. And "What is't to me," he asks, when the citizens of Harfleur have, by their obstinacy, brought this scourge upon themselves. He bids the governor take pity on the young girls, the old men, and the infants, and yield to the clemency offered by the king.

## Comment

There are both practical and ethical reasons why Henry prefers that Harfleur surrender rather than be sacked. We already know that he wishes to be merciful as far as he can, and that he abhors the thought of rape and plunder. Moreover, like any good general, he realizes the importance of discipline in his army, and he knows that his hold over his men is not absolute. Once they get out of control, as they are likely to do when they sack Harfleur, they will become a less effective fighting force for the future. For both these reasons he hopes for the surrender of the city.

Henry makes this declaration on his honor as a soldier, "A name that in my thoughts becomes me best." We may recall this remark when in the fifth act he woos Katherine with the words, "take me, take a soldier; take a soldier, take a king." For Shakespeare an ideal king must be a great soldier. Queen Elizabeth, although she could not fight in battle with her troops, used to ride with them to the front. Henry really was an excellent soldier. In *Henry IV* Part I we witnessed his victory over Hotspur at Shrewsbury. History tells us that at the Battle of Agincourt, which takes place in the fourth act, he killed the Duke of Alençon in combat. In the play, however, his encounter with Alençon is referred to only in passing. Why did Shakespeare leave this out? We can only conclude that Shakespeare did not want to stress the heroic feats that Henry may have performed. Instead, he concentrated on the other qualities that make an outstanding general: bravery, devotion to his cause, a spirit of companionship with his men, and the ability to inspire confidence.

The governor agrees to yield the town, for he has received word from the Dauphin that reinforcements cannot arrive in time. Henry gives his uncle Exeter command of Harfleur with orders to fortify it and to treat its citizens with mercy. With winter coming on and sickness spreading among the troops, Henry will spend only one night in Harfleur before withdrawing with the army to Calais.

## Comment

The English have made an excellent beginning to the war, but their prospects for the future are not altogether rosy, for the army is much weakened. Henry plans to march on to Calais if he can, to rest and recuperate. The port of Calais on the French side of the English Channel was taken by the English under Edward the Third and remained an English stronghold until the middle of the sixteenth century. We will shortly see that Henry was forced to fight at Agincourt before he could reach Calais.

Henry's command that Exeter be merciful to the citizens of Harfleur is in accordance with what we know of his temperament.

### SUMMARY

In this short scene we learn:

1. Harfleur falls to the English because reinforcements cannot be sent in time.

2. Henry prefers that the town surrender than that it be sacked in battle.

3. He will treat the citizens with mercy.

4. The English hope to rest for a while in Calais, for their strength has been sapped by sickness.

## ACT III: SCENE 4

This short scene takes place in a room in the French palace and is mainly in French. Princess Katherine tells her lady in waiting, Alice, that she would like to learn to speak English, and asks Alice, who has been in England, to teach her some words. Repeating after her maid, Katherine learns to say hand, fingers, nails, elbow, neck, chin, foot, and gown. Each time she learns a new word she reviews all the others. Both teacher and pupil make comical mistakes in pronunciation. Alice, for example, says "nick" for "neck" and Katherine says "bilbow" for elbow and "sin" for "chin." At one point, after Katherine has just mispronounced five words in a row, Alice compliments her for speaking like a native. At the end of this short lesson the princess has mastered nine words of English.

### Comment

This scene is lighthearted and amusing. Katherine, a charming young lady, evidently understands that she may become queen of England and she seems to take that prospect in her stride. Some mistakes in pronunciation are particularly funny because they pun on French slang words. Alice pronounces "foot" and "gown" in such a way that they sound like words that no young French girl would ever say in public. We may wonder how large a part of Shakespeare's original audience understood French. We cannot be sure of the answer but probably many commoners as well as all the gentry understood the elementary French used in this scene. The others could easily follow the general meaning, since Alice and Katherine undoubtedly pointed to the different parts of the body as they said the words in French and in heavily accented English.

**SUMMARY**

> This scene gives us a first glimpse of the charming Katherine and provides some humor to lighten the play. In the fifth act we will see what progress she makes with her English.

## ACT III: SCENE 5

The king of France, the Dauphin, the Constable, the Duke of Britaine (called Bourbon in some editions), and others are in conference in Rouen (a city not far from Harfleur in northern France). The king declares that Henry has surely passed the river Somme by now. The others, angry and humiliated at the recent developments in the invasion, begin reviling England and the English. What are these upstarts but "Norman bastards," asks Britaine. (In 1066 the Normans under William the Conqueror defeated the Saxons and took control of England. Gradually the ruling Normans mixed with the native Saxons to produce a new race of Englishmen.) The duke declares that if the English are allowed to advance unopposed, he will buy a dirty farm in the shabby isle of Albion. (Albion was another name for England, generally derogatory.) The Constable wonders where the English get their daring spirit, since the English climate is raw and foggy and the English sun rarely shines. How can a people whose national drink is beer compare with the wine drinking French. "O for the honor of our land," he cries, let us show ourselves the equal of these "frosty English." The Dauphin and Britaine say that the French ladies mock their lords as cowards, and bid them learn to dance in English dancing schools, since the only step they seem to know is how to run away.

## Comment

The French are mortified that Henry has advanced so far unimpeded. Their bitter mockery of the English ancestry, climate, and drink is a way of venting anger and expressing contempt for the enemy, whom they are eager to confront. We, of course, know that the English will prove to be more than a match for the sneering French.

After hearing these speeches, the king sends for his herald, Montjoy, that he may send a message of sharp defiance to the English. Ordering the dukes, princes, barons, lords, and knights to the field, he bids them wipe away the stain of the English invasion and bring Henry prisoner to Rouen. This royal declaration satisfies the Constable. He declares that he is only sorry that the English army is so small and its soldiers sick and hungry, for he is sure that Henry will shrink with fear and offer ransom instead of fighting. Seizing upon this idea, the king orders the herald to ask Henry what ransom he will voluntarily offer to avoid a battle. Then, commanding the unwilling Dauphin to remain with him in Rouen, the king sends the Constable and other lords to meet the English.

## Comment

The king's indignation at the fall of Harfleur is further aroused by the bitter words spoken by the noblemen. He is determined to stop the English advance with no delay. The French know that the English army has been considerably weakened by sickness, and they think that Henry will prefer to offer ransom rather than fight. We shall see later in the play how unjust an estimate this is of Henry's character.

The king expressly orders the Dauphin to remain in Rouen. According to history, the Dauphin was not present at Agincourt, but later in the act we shall see that Shakespeare preferred to represent him as having joined the battle in disobedience of his father's command.

### SUMMARY

In this scene we learn two facts about the French:

1. They are still derisive of the English, but now they are also furious and humiliated.

2. They plan to bar Henry's further passage through the land without more delay. If he will not offer ransom, they will initiate the fighting. They are confident of success.

## ACT III: SCENE 6

The scene is near Agincourt, the day before the battle. Captains Gower and Fluellen meet on stage. Fluellen, who has just come from the bridge which he calls the Pridge), expresses his admiration for the excellent disciplined maintained there by the Duke of Exeter, who is in charge. At the bridge he noticed in particular one soldier named Pistol, who seemed as valiant as Mark Anthony. Just at this moment, in comes the same Pistol, looking for Fluellen. Bardolph, it seems, has stolen a pax from a church (a pax is a holy tablet kissed by communicants during Mass) and is sentenced to be hanged. In his usual absurd way, Pistol declares that fortune has turned against Bardolph. Fluellen, who likes the sound of his own voice quite as much as Pistol does his, gives his own account of the fickle goddess

HENRY V

fortune and the moral that she holds for men. However, when Pistol begs Fluellen to use his influence with the Duke of Exeter to save Bardolph, the Welshman refuses outright. Even if the culprit were his own brother, says Fluellen, "discipline ought to be used." Pistol answers by cursing Fluellen, and repeating the vulgar expression "figo" and "the fig of Spain" before he exits. (These terms were accompanied by a gesture of contempt, putting the thumb between two closed fingers or into the mouth.)

Despite Fluellen's assurance that he heard Pistol speak brave words at the bridge, Gower declares that Pistol is a notorious rascal, pander, and thief, the kind of man who follows the army during a war in order to play the part of a hero when he returns to London. Such a man will avoid all danger and concentrate upon learning the names of the generals, and who fought at which places in order to impress his gullible friends in the tavern at home. Fluellen sees that he was taken in by Pistol's bravado, but he promises to unmask the rascal at the first opportunity. At this point the king enters. Fluellen must give him news of the bridge.

Comment

It is proof of Fluellen's naiveté that he was taken in by Pistol's blustering words at the bridge. When we hear that braggart's absurdly pompous manner of speech we realize that Fluellen, if he were a little more clever, would have suspected him from the moment he opened his mouth. If Fluellen is comical in some ways, he is, nevertheless, to be admired for his insistence on the impartial and stern enforcement of discipline in the army. His promise to seek a quarrel with Pistol, unlike his proposed debate with Captain Macmorris, will be fulfilled later in the play. Pistol is a buffoon, and we cannot help laughing at him;

but Bardolph's thievery is no joke. We have been prepared for it by the Boy's soliloquy in the second scene, and we have also been led to expect the enforcement of discipline in the English army. In the fifteenth and sixteenth centuries, the death penalty was normally imposed for minor felonies. Theft of a religious object such as a pax was a serious matter, for it involved sacrilege. An Elizabethan audience would, therefore, not have considered Bardolph's sentence unduly harsh, although we in the twentieth century may find it excessive.

Gower's remark that Pistol has joined the army in order to pass himself off as a veteran in London will prove to hit the mark exactly. In the fifth act we will see that Pistol intends to do just that.

Fluellen tells the king that after some fighting the French have withdrawn and the brave Duke of Exeter is master of the bridge. Whereas the enemy suffered numerous casualties, the English lost only Bardolph, who is to be executed for robbing a church. The king declares, "We would have all such offenders so cut off." He gives orders that in the course of the English march through the countryside nothing is to be taken without being justly paid for and none of the French are to be abused in word or deed. When gentleness and cruelty contend for a kingdom, he says, lenience is the more likely winner.

## Comment

In *Henry IV* Part I Prince Hal and Bardolph were comrades for a while. Fluellen's description of the thief makes it quite certain that he is the same man. But Henry gives no sign of recognition. Like Fuellen he believes that discipline must be strictly enforced.

Henry realizes that the less he antagonizes the French, the less resistance they will offer and the easier his passage through the countryside will be. Moreover, because he hopes to be king of France as well as England, he wants to win the confidence and the respect of the French people. A policy of gentleness, therefore, is both good morals and good politics.

Montjoy, the French herald, enters with his message for Henry. The French king sends word that up to now he has been biding his time. He could have stopped Henry at Harfluer if he had wanted to, but he chose to wait and make deliberate preparations. Now he bids Henry consider what ransom he will offer, although all the wealth of England cannot compensate for the loss of French blood and the stain on the French honor. Sending his defiance, the French king warns that the fate of the English is sealed.

After complimenting the herald on the ability with which he performs his office, Henry answers that although he would willingly march on to Calais without a battle, he will not avoid one. His few men are so weak and sickly, he says, that they are "almost no better than so many French." When they were in health, he declares, he thought one Englishman the equal of three French. Stopping himself short for bragging, the king asks God to forgive him. It is the French air that has blown this vice in him, he affirms, and he must repent. Rejecting the very thought of ransom, he bids Montjoy tell his master: "My ransom is this frail and worthless trunk; / My army but a weak and sickly guard; / Yet, God before, tell him we will come on, / Though France herself and such another neighbor / Stand in our way." He gives the herald a purse for his labor, and Montjoy, promising to deliver the message, departs. When he has gone, the Duke of Gloucester says he hopes the French will not seek a battle now, to which the king replies, "We are in God's hand, brother, not in theirs." He orders that the army camp for the night across the bridge.

## Comment

Henry knows that a wise general does not tell the enemy of his weakness, but he also knows that the condition of his troops is no secret from the French. (In the previous scene we learned that the French know perfectly well that the invading army has been greatly weakened.) There is no harm in letting them know that he would rather get on safely to Calais. If they insist upon fighting, he is ready to meet them.

Until about the eighteenth century, ransom was practiced instead of an exchange of prisoners of war. When noblemen (and especially kings) were captured, they were held prisoner until their family and countrymen raised a large enough sum of money to buy their freedom. Common soldiers, who could not command such fortunes, seldom lived to return home once they were taken prisoner. Henry's refusal to offer ransom for himself is tantamount to an avowal that he will share the fate of his men, no matter what the outcome of the encounter with the French.

Montjoy is an effective herald, for he eloquently represents the French king in his message of defiance. It is characteristic of Henry that he acknowledges Montjoy's ability, giving praise and largess where it is due, even to one of the enemy. It is even more characteristic of Henry that he repents of bragging about his men to the French herald. A king should have more self-control. Finally, we feel the conviction with which Henry believes that he is in the hands of God. The French threat is nothing to him if God is on his side.

## SUMMARY

In this scene we learn the following things:

1. Bardolph has been sentenced to death for stealing a pax from a church. Pistol tries to have Fluellen intervene with the Duke of Exeter on his behalf, but the Welshman refuses. Discipline must be enforced.

2. The English have driven the French from the bridge and will therefore be able to camp on the other side of the stream that night.

3. Henry believes that gentleness will win a country sooner than cruelty.

4. The herald delivers the French king's message of defiance, and Henry replies that he will never offer ransom. If the French will not let him pass on to Calais, he will stand and fight.

5. Henry is not the kind of man to brag. If he finds himself tending to do so, he will stifle the impulse. His confidence in the outcome of an encounter with the French is based on faith in God as well as in his men.

## ACT III: SCENE 7

It is the eve of the battle. Several French lords are whiling away the hours in desultory conversation. The Constable brags of his armor, Orleans of his horse, and all long for morning. The Dauphin begins to praise his horse with romantic fervor:

"He trots the air. The earth sings when he touches it. The basest horn of his hoof is more musical than the pipe of Hermes." Once the Dauphin wrote a **sonnet** to his horse beginning, 'Wonder of nature." The others remark that such language is usually reserved for one's mistress, and the Dauphin replies "my horse is my mistress," a statement that gives his companions a **theme** for puns and double meanings. For example, the Constable says he would just as soon have his mistress a jade (jade means both a horse and a loose woman). Deriding the English, Rambures offers to go hazard with anyone for twenty prisoners. At midnight the Dauphin goes off to arm himself, and the others, who remain behind, make him the subject of conversation. The Constable has a low opinion of the Dauphin, for he brags too much about his horse and his valor and about what he will do to the English. Orleans defends the Dauphin as a gallant prince, but the Constable insists that no one ever witnessed his bravery except his servant (whom he can treat with impunity anyway).

## Comment

The French, unlike the English, are not led by one outstanding man who commands all their respect. Although the Dauphin is the heir apparent to the throne and therefore the ranking prince at this gathering, he is the least respected man present. His encomiums upon his horse are ridiculously exaggerated and are made the butt of jokes. His protestations of valor on the battlefield are doubted by the others and infer that he has never shown courage in the past and there is no reason to think that he is about to change his ways. Whereas Henry tries to restrain whatever impulse he may feel to brag about his men (as in the last scene), the Dauphin is a confirmed braggart.

The French lords are in the midst of matching proverbs with one another when a messenger comes in to tell the Constable that the distance between the enemy camps is fifteen hundred paces. The Constable thinks "Poor Harry of England" does not long for the morning as the French do, and Orleans agrees that if the English had any sense at all, they would run away. Rambures declares that the English mastiffs are very brave, but Orleans maintains that it is foolishness and not bravery to fight against overwhelming odds. The Constable agrees that the English must have left their wits at home with their wives. Now it is time to arm. By ten o'clock, he prophesies, "We shall each have a hundred Englishmen."

Comment

In the following act we will contrast the serious mood of the English with the frivolous temper of the French on this battle eve. For the time being, we merely note that the French are spending their time making bawdy jokes and belittling the English. The **irony** of the scene is that we know that "Poor Harry" and the English soldiers are on the eve of a great victory.

**SUMMARY**

This scene shows:

1. The French feel little respect for their titular leader who, in fact, seems to merit none at all.

2. The French feel confident of victory and underestimate the power of their adversary.

# HENRY V

## TEXTUAL ANALYSIS

## ACT 4

### ACT IV: SCENE 1

The Chorus sets the scene by describing the sights and sounds of the army camps the night before the battle of Agincourt. The two armies are so close to each other that each sentinel can almost hear his opposite whispering the password. In the light of the flickering fires, each side glimpses the faces of the enemy. Sounds are heard through the night of horses neighing and of armorers closing up the rivets on the knights (who had to be encased in ponderously heavy battle armor). Cocks crow. It is three in the morning. The French, confident of victory, are impatient for the day to begin. The haggard English, fearfully sitting by their fires, "Sit patiently and inly ruminate / The morning's danger." Henry, "The royal captain of this ruined band," walks throughout his camp to inspect and to cheer his soldiers. He "Bids them good morrow with a modest smile / And calls them brothers, friends, and countrymen. / Upon his royal face there is no note /

How dread an army hath enrounded him." Henry appears so unwearied and untroubled that the apprehensive soldiers are heartened by the "little touch of Harry in the night."

The Chorus concludes with apologies for presuming to represent the great battle of Agincourt with a handful of actors on a stage.

## Comment

This speech contains some of the best poetry in the play. We are made to hear the sounds and see the sights of that long night by means of the vivid language of the Chorus. We learn that the English are afraid, as they have every right to be, but that Henry manages to put courage in their hearts.

Conferring with his two brothers. Gloucester and Bedford, during the grim night, the king tries to persuade them that good can sometimes be derived from the worst of situations. He encourages them to think of the enemy as unwittingly doing them a service, by making them rise early, which is healthful and prudent, and by causing them to summon up their reserves of courage. Moreover, the French threat results in the English preparing their souls for death and examining their consciences, which is also very good to do and all too often neglected.

Sir Thomas Erpingham, a loyal and white-haired captain, enters. Cheerfully he tells the king that he is quite content where he is, "Since I may say, 'Now lie I like a king.'" These brave words please the king greatly. Telling the others that he wishes to be alone for a while, he borrows a cloak from the good old man, and the others leave him.

## Comment

Henry is determined to put a cheerful face on things. Whatever fears he may have he does not reveal to his closest friends, his brothers, any more than to the common soldiers. Unlike the French lords, whom we saw in the last act, the English are thoughtful and serious on the eve of battle, which is natural enough since their prospects are very grim. But the difference in mood is also indicative of the fundamental differences in character that Shakespeare intends to suggest between the French and the English.

Pistol enters and, noticing the king (who is disguised by his cloak) he demands, "Qui va la?" (In French this means: who goes there? In Elizabethan England thieves commonly used this phrase among themselves.) Henry identifies himself as a Welsh gentleman named Harry le Roy. (Le roi, in French, means the king; and Henry, born in Monmouth, was therefore Welsh by birth.) When Pistol asks the stranger if he knows Fluellen, the king answers that he not only knows Fluellen but is his friend and kinsman. Pistol then bids him warn Fluellen of his intention to knock his leek about his head upon Saint Davy's day.

## Comment

The leek is the national emblem of Wales. It was customary among the Welsh to wear a leek in their hats on Saint Davy's day, March 1st, to celebrate the anniversary of their victory over the Saxons. We gather from this threat that Pistol intends to persist in his grudge against Fluellen for refusing to help Bardolph. Throughout this encounter, Pistol addresses the unknown gentleman with his customary insolence and bravado. Yet when asked about the king, he reveals nothing but admiration and affection for the monarch, although he expresses his feelings in unduly familiar language.

After Pistol exits, the king remains on stage and overhears Gower and Fluellen, who pass by. Fluellen is reprimanding Gower for speaking in a loud tone of voice. He declares in his usual longwinded sentences that it is strictly against the ancient rules of warfare to make such noise, and that Pompey would never have allowed it. Gower objects that the enemy is very noisy, but Fluellen replies indignantly, "If the enemy is an ass and a fool and a prating coxcomb, is it meet, think you, that we should also, look you, be an ass and a fool and a prating coxcomb?" Gower agrees to speak lower, and the two captains exit. The king is pleased with Fluellen's carefulness and valor, even though the Welshman is "a little out of fashion."

Comment

Like Sir Thomas Epringham, Fluellen is a loyal and cheerful captain in this trying hour. His adamant insistence on what he believes to be the **conventions** of ancient warfare as well as his quaint ways of talking are amusing in the manner of gentle satire.

Three soldiers enter next: John Bates, Alexander Court, and Michael Williams, all worried about the coming battle. The king tells them that he belongs to the company of Sir Thomas Erpingham who, he says, in answer to their question, has refrained from telling the king his fears. This is as it should be, continues Henry, for "I think the king is but a man, as I am. The violet smells to him as it doth to me; all his senses have but human conditions. His ceremonies laid by, in his nakedness he appears but a man." Since the king is as liable to fears as any man, it is important that no one should encourage his apprehension, "lest he, by showing it, should dishearten his army."

Bates declares that no matter what courage the king may display, he probably wishes himself anywhere else than here. Henry denies such a suggestion. He thinks the king would not want to be anywhere else. Speaking for himself then, Bates wishes he were safely out of this trap. Henry affirms that he would gladly die in the king's just and honorable cause. Bates replies that subjects cannot know and should not seek to judge the merits of a king's cause. Then, if the king be wrong, he alone is responsible for the misdeeds committed in his name.

Williams ponders this question. If the king leads men to their death in battle for an unjust cause, he will have a heavy responsibility to fear, especially for those who die with souls unshriven and unprepared for the last judgment. Henry strongly objects to this argument. He declares that the king is no more responsible for the state of his subjects, souls when they die in battle than the father is responsible for the soul of his son who drowns at sea while on his father's business. The king does not intend his subjects' death while they are in his service. Besides, no army is without soldiers who have sinned, and in some cases war is God's way of catching and punishing the guilty. "Every subject's duty is the king's, but every subject's soul is his own." Therefore, every soldier should settle his account with God and his own conscience before a battle, just as a sick man should do. Then, if he dies, he will die well, and if he lives, he will enjoy an easy conscience and a state of grace. Williams and Bates are convinced by this argument, and they resolve to fight lustily for the king. Henry declares that he heard the king say he would not be ransomed, but Williams is sceptical about the durability of that promise. It is all very well for the king to say what he pleases before the battle, but when the soldiers' throats are cut he may be ransomed all the same. At this Henry becomes indignant. He vows that if he lives to see it, he will never trust the king's word after. Williams becomes even more scornful at this remark. What can it injure a monarch, he demands, if a subject does not trust his word? A monarch is impervious to the displeasure of a commoner. The king, angry at this reproof, exchanges a glove with Williams as a gage. After battle, if they are living, Williams will wear Henry's glove in his hat and Henry promises to challenge it, warning that he may "take thee in the king's company." Bates urges the two adversaries to be friends. The English have enough quarrels with the French, he says, without squabbling among themselves. The soldiers depart, leaving Henry alone on the stage.

## Comment

This encounter is particularly interesting because it reveals the attitudes of the common soldiers. The rest of the play deals with the actions and thoughts of the nobility, and of the gentry such as Captain Fluellen, and of rascals such as Pistol. Here, for the first time we glimpse the character and feelings of the ordinary soldier, who does not know what the war is about and does not seek to know. Of the three soldiers, Williams is the most interesting because he raises the question of the king's responsibility for the souls of the men who die in battle. Henry's answer satisfies the men on this score. Every subject is responsible for his own soul. We must understand this discussion in its historical context. Political theory of the fifteenth and sixteenth centuries was based on the concept of the divine right of kings, according to which the king was accepted as God's agent on earth, responsible for his actions only to God and not to his subjects. In all circumstances the duty of the subject is to obey the king. None of the soldiers ever questions this concept. Whereas a modern American or European soldier may very well feel that it is his business to understand and approve of the cause for which he is fighting, these soldiers are not accustomed to making judgments on the decisions of their rulers. We may note in this connection that Henry never discusses with the men the reasons why the king's cause is just and honorable. Perhaps this is because questions of national honor and territorial expansion really would not matter to these simple men.

Another difference between contemporary and Elizabethan society is that the sixteenth century was thoroughly convinced of the validity of religious concepts of the last judgment and of life after death. It is not very likely that a modern soldier would hold the leader of his country responsible for the soldier's immortal soul, as Williams suggests the king is. It is far more likely that the modern soldier would ask instead whether the ruler is not to blame for depriving men of life on earth. That is, the twentieth century places a far greater emphasis on this world than on the next. The question Williams asks, however, and the question Henry answers is about the soldier's soul and not his body.

Because the soldiers do not recognize the king, they treat him with the easy familiarity of an equal, and it is for this reason that the quarrel develops between Henry and Williams. The king is not used to blunt rebukes. His high position shields him from insulting words, except occasionally from a hostile prince like the Dauphin. Moreover, he is angry that Williams is sceptical of his promise to refuse to be ransomed. The soldier's reasoning is logical enough, for he could not be sure that the king would not change his mind and break his oath. But Henry takes this scepticism as an insult to his honor, and he is very sensitive on this score. That is why he makes an issue of it. If the two adversaries were of equal rank, the exchange of gage would be quite natural. However, a fight between a commoner and the king is absolutely unthinkable. We will see at the end of the act how the quarrel is resolved.

Left to his thoughts, Henry soliloquizes on the burdens of the kingship, "We must bear all." Musing upon his conversation with the soldiers, he notes that subjects try to lay all their responsibilities upon the king for their lives, souls, debts, wives, children, and sins. The king can never enjoy privacy such as the ordinary man knows, for his name, his words, and all his actions are the task of every fool. "And what have kings that privates have not too, / Save ceremony, save general ceremony?"

And what, after all, is the value of ceremony? It brings in no rents. In fact, it is nothing but "place, degree and form / Creating fear in other men." And those other men are more happy fearing the king than he is in being feared, for he can never be sure that friendship will not turn to betrayal (we recall Scroop). Ceremony and all the accoutrements of royalty (the balm, the sceptre, the sword, the crown, the royal robes, the throne) cannot cure the sick nor even teach the king to sleep as soundly as a wretched peasant who, toiling from sunrise to sunset, "Sleeps in Elysium." Except for ceremony the peasant has the advantage over the king. His days occupied with profitable labor, the peasant never guesses what work it is for the king to maintain the country's peace.

## Comment

This is Henry's most developed soliloquy in the play. It is the first time we hear him thinking rather than talking to others, and therefore it is our first and most direct glimpse of the "man" within the "king." We are prepared for this speech by his words to the soldiers. When he tells them that "the king is but a man," we realize that we are seeing a new side to Henry's character. So far we have only seen how admirably he suits the office of the king. Now we become aware of how keenly he feels his mortality and the burdens of the kingship. It is at this moment that

Henry's complexity begins to approach that of a tragic figure whose soul is in conflict. At this moment he feels that ceremony, mere external show, is not worth the sacrifice of peace of mind. This mood does not last long. In a few minutes Henry will be himself again, but in the meantime we have been reminded of one of the important **themes** of the play: the human dimension of Henry's kingship.

Sir Thomas Erpingham enters and, finding Henry, tells him that the English nobles are seeking him throughout the camp. The king agrees to meet them at his tent. When Erpingham leaves, the king prays to God to keep his men free from fear when they will see the numbers of the enemy. He beseeches God not to remember on this day that his father Henry IV, acquired the crown by deposing Richard II. To atone for his father's crime, the son has given Richard new burial and has built two chapels where priests sing mass for Richard's soul. Moreover, the king keeps in his service five hundred paupers to pray for forgiveness of his father's sin, and he himself sheds contrite tears of penitence for that deed. Gloucester comes upon the king at this moment and Henry goes off with him, declaring. "The day, my friends, and all things stay for me."

### Comment

In the earlier play *Richard II,* Shakespeare described how Henry Bolingbroke deposed his cousin Richard and became king Henry IV. Richard was imprisoned and later he was murdered by someone who thought he was doing the new king a favor. However, Henry IV repudiated the murderer and condemned the deed. In the play *Henry IV,* the king plans to go on a holy pilgrimage to expiate the sin of Richard's deposition and murder, but he is prevented from going by civil wars at home.

In this scene we see that Henry V has not forgotten the crime that brought his father to the throne. It is interesting that these thoughts should occur to him immediately after talking with the three soldiers about the duty all subjects owe to the king. Henry's own father defied the divinely ordained position of King Richard II and was implicated in regicide, the greatest crime a subject can commit.

Henry was doubtless deeply troubled by his father's deed, not only for ethical reasons but also because it weakened his own claim to the English throne. It is said that Queen Elizabeth objected to the play Richard II because she did not want her subjects to be reminded of a successful deposition of the lawful king. She felt it tended to undermine the absolute authority of the monarchy. Similarly, Henry preferred that this subjects did not think of how his father came to be king. But even more, he did not want God to punish the son (himself) for the sins of the father. The justification for Henry's war against France was his legal claim to the French throne. This is the only reference in the play to Henry's right to be king of England.

**SUMMARY**

This scene is the high point of the play for several reasons.

1. We learn that the English are fearful of the coming battle but resolved to fight as valiantly as they can. Henry fulfills his role as commander in chief by visiting with his troops and cheering his men.

2. Pistol's threat to knock the leek about Fluellen's head on Saint Davy's day prepares us for what takes place in the first scene of act five.

3. Fluellen reappears briefly, quaint but undoubtedly loyal to the bottom of his heart.

4. Most important of all, we are reminded that the king is a man, with hopes and fears and loves like any other man. Because most of the play shows Henry as a king in office, the encounter with the three soldiers and the following soliloquy are essential to complete our understanding of Henry as a human being.

5. The three soldiers, in their conversation, give us an idea of how the average Englishman in Henry's army was thinking and feeling that night.

6. Henry's quarrel with Williams prepares us for further action in the last scene of their act.

7. We are reminded of how Henry IV came to the throne and of Henry's awareness of the crime his father committed.

8. We see that Henry is devout in private as well as in public. His prayers for God's favor are sincere and from the heart.

## ACT IV: SCENE 2

It is morning. Several French lords, including the Dauphin, Orleans, and the Constable, are preparing to mount their horses. They are in high spirits and joke about the tears the English soon will be shedding. A messenger arrives to tell them that the enemy is already on the battlefield. Surveying the poor and ragged

English army, the Constable declares that the French lackeys and peasants could defeat such a rabble. Grandpre agrees, for the English banners are so shabby, their horses so sickly, and their general appearance so lifeless that he refers to the English as "Yond island carrions, desperate of their bones." Finally, after the Dauphin laughingly suggests giving the enemy fresh suits and a decent meal, the French depart for the battlefield.

Comment And Summary:

This is the last time we shall see the French so confident and scornful. They will make no more jokes at the expense of the English army. The **irony** of this scene, as of all previous scenes depicting the French, is that we know what the outcome of the battle will be.

## ACT IV: SCENE 3

The English lords are gathered together, awaiting Henry's return from inspecting the battlefield. Westmoreland says that the enemy has 30,000 men, or about five times as many as the English. The lords bid each other farewell. A spirit of harmony and friendship pervades the somber group, as they wish each other good luck and praise each other for valor and kindness.

As the king enters he overhears Westmoreland wishing for 10,000 more English soldiers, a wish that Henry does not share. Turning from Westmoreland to address all his troops, the king declares that he does not wish a single additional man. "If we are marked to die, we are enow / To do our country loss; and if to live, / The fewer men, the greater share of honor." He says that though he is not greedy for money, he is covetous of honor and, therefore, he does not want to share the honor of this glorious battle with a single additional man. Moreover, he does not want anyone to fight with him who does so in fear and against his will. Henry tells Westmoreland to proclaim throughout the army that any soldier who wants to leave will be given a passport and money for the journey. "We would not die in that man's company / That fears his fellowship to die with us." This day is the Feast of Saint Crispin, he reminds his listeners. Looking into the future, he foresees that on the anniversary of this day each soldier who survives the battle will celebrate, feasting his neighbors and telling them what feats he did on Crispin's day. Each man shall tell his son, and the sons will tell their sons, so that throughout history this glorious day will live in the minds of men. "We few, we happy few, we band of brothers; / For he today that sheds his blood with me / Shall gentle his condition; / And gentlemen in England now abed / Shall think themselves accursed they were not here, / And held their manhood cheap while any speaks / That fought with us upon Saint Crispin's day."

## Comment

The oratory of this speech is superb. No army could fail to thrill to its stirring words. What makes it so effective? The answer, in large measure, is that Henry makes his soldiers feel that it is a privilege rather than a disagreeable duty to fight in the coming battle. He knows that his men are afraid and that they have every reason to be afraid. He does not attempt to minimize the danger, nor does he talk about the justice of his cause. His appeal is based entirely on the desire for honor that each soldier must be feeling. Under the spell of his oratory the English army is no longer 5,000 desperate individuals but a "band of brothers," all zealous for fame and glory. As a result of this day's work, he promises, their names and deeds will be remembered and honored throughout history.

Salisbury re-enters with news that the French are ready. Westmoreland, fired by the king's rousing words, declares that he wishes he and Henry could take on the enemy by themselves. Henry's speech has clearly infused the English with courage and enthusiasm.

Trumpets sound and Montjoy appears on behalf of the Constable to ask Henry once more if he will offer ransom and prevent certain defeat. The Constable also bids him remind his troops to settle the state of their souls, for they will surely die upon this field. Henry's answer is defiance and refusal to offer ransom. Why should they mock me thus? he wonders. "The man that once did sell the lion's skin / While the beast lived, was killed with hunting him." Henry tells the herald proudly that he and his men are tried and tested warriors. Their uniforms, once fresh and new, are now soiled from days of marching through French fields. Managing to joke in this trying hour, he says that the lack of feathers in their head-gear should be a sign that they will not fly (double meaning: they will neither fly like a bird nor run away). Inside these ragged uniforms, he tells the herald, "our hearts are in the trim," for the English have determined to wrest new clothes from the defeated French. Henry tells Montjoy never to come again on such an errand, for the king will offer no ransom but his own dead body. The herald departs, promising not to return. The Duke of York begs Henry that he may lead the vanguard of the troops and the king agrees, bidding his soldiers march away, "And how thou pleasest, God, dispose the day."

Comment

Henry is angered by the visit from the herald, which he considers an insult to his honor. He is a man of his word, and he has already declared his intention not to be ransomed. Like the soldier

Williams, however, the French appear to think that he might change his mind. We see that his resolution holds firm, as he relies, as always, upon divine providence to determine the outcome.

### SUMMARY

This scene is important for the following reasons:

1. We learn that the English are outnumbered by five to one and they know it. In this hour of danger, the English lords show courage and loving friendship in bidding each other farewell.

2. Henry delivers a thrilling speech of encouragement to his soldiers, appealing to their sense of honor and desire for glory. We feel certain that the army is heartened by his words.

3. The French herald, Montjoy, reappears and offers Henry one last chance to be ransomed. The king, however, is faithful to his word, and sends Montjoy back with a message of defiance.

4. The Duke of York shows his zeal by asking permission to lead the first line of troops. We will see later how he fared on the battlefield.

## ACT IV: SCENE 4

This short and comparatively lighthearted scene takes place in the middle of the battle of Agincourt. Pistol has captured a French soldier. The soldier begs for mercy in French, and Pistol demands money in English, and neither one understand the other. Finally, the Boy undertakes to translate. He discovers that the soldier's name is Mr. Fer, that he comes from a good family, and that he will give Pistol two hundred crowns for his ransom. This offer satisfies Pistol, and the soldier expresses his thankfulness for having fallen into the hands of one whom he calls, "them sot brave, valorous, and thrice-worthy seigneur of England." Pistol and his captive exit. The Boy, left alone on stage, declares that he never heard so much noise come from such an empty heart as Pistol's. Nym and Bardolph, who have both been hanged, at least had more courage than Pistol. The Boy says that he must stay with the other lackeys with the baggage of the camp, which the French could easily capture, since it is guarded only by boys.

Comment And Summary:

We may deduce from the fact that Pistol has captured a French prisoner either that the French are utterly routed or that this particular French soldier is a complete coward. The humor of this scene results from the absurdity of the situation: Pistol lording it over a prisoner. We know Pistol too well to be taken in by his swaggering pose of the conquering hero. The other element of comedy is confusion over languages, particularly when a French word sounds like an English word with an entirely different meaning. For example, when the soldier says "bras" (French for "arm"), Pistol thinks he is offering brass instead of gold. The Boy's speech at the end prepares us for what will happen in the baggage train of the English army later in the act.

## ACT IV: SCENE 5

The Constable, the Dauphin, Orleans, Bourbon, and Rambures, realizing that they have lost the battle, cry shame upon themselves. Is this the king we sent to for his ransom, they ask. Are these the English for whom we played at dice? Determined to make one last attempt to save their honor if not the battle, they return to be field in the same disorder as before. "Let life be short; else shame will be too long."

## Comment And Summary

Except for a brief scuffle between Pistol and his prisoner in the previous scene, we never see any fighting on stage. Thus we learn how the battle is going by hearing the French talk among themselves, not by actually witnessing their defeat. At last they have come to realize the caliber of the English, and retract their contemptuous remarks. For the first time we see the French acting and not just talking about honor. In the face of disaster they rush back to the fray. If they have been foolish before, at least they are not cowardly now.

## ACT IV: SCENES 6 AND 7

Although the English have done well, the fighting is not yet over, the king tells his followers, for the French are still in the field. Exeter brings word that the Duke of York, died in battle. He describes how the fatally wounded York stretched out bedside the Earl of Suffolk, who had just died, and embracing his friend, declared that he was glad that their two souls would fly to heaven together, "As in this glorious and well-foughten field / We kept together in our chivalry" York's last words were "Commend my service to my sovereign." Exeter admits that he was moved to tears by this scene, and the king is equally touched by this description.

An alarm announces that the French have reorganized their scattered men to make a last stand. Henry orders all prisoners to be killed.

### Comment

York represents the ideal chivalric knight. He is a loyal subject and a devoted friend to the death. We remember that he asked Henry earlier for permission to lead the vanguard. Now we learn that he fought valiantly and died nobly.

Henry orders that the prisoners be killed because of the French rally. We will see in the next scene that another reason for this decision is given by Gower.

## SCENE 7

Fluellen and Gower are aghast that the French have attacked the English baggage train, killing all the boys and burning the king's tent. It is certain that there is not a boy left alive. Therefore, says Gower, the king, in reprisal, has caused his soldiers to kill their prisoners. He praises the king for this, "O, 'tis a gallant king."

### Comment

In the previous scene we heard Henry give the order for killing prisoners because he saw the French rally on the field. Now, however, we are told that he made this decision only after the French contravened the laws of war and of humanity by killing the boys, who were noncombatants. If we thought that the order was needlessly cruel when we heard it in the previous scene, perhaps we feel it is slightly more explicable now that we know what the French have done. In any case, it is clear that Henry's captains approve of his retaliatory action.

We must remember at this point that the Boy said in the fourth scene that he was going to stay with the luggage. He was undoubtedly killed with all the others in the French raid.

Fluellen compares Henry to Alexander the Great, whom he calls Alexander the Pig (it is one of his peculiarities to say "p" for "b"). Macedon, Alexander's birthplace, and Monmouth, Henry's birthplace, are almost identical, says Fluellen. At Monmouth there is a river called the Wye and at Macedon there is also a river, although he cannot remember its name. "But 'tis all one; 'tis alike as my fingers is to my fingers." Then, comparing Henry's life with Alexander's, he says that Alexander, when he was drunk and angry, killed his best friend Cleitus. Gower interrupts to deny any similarity between Henry and Alexander on that score, for Henry never killed any of his friends. But Fluellen explains that he meant to compare the way that Alexander in a drunken rage killed Cleitus with the way that Henry, "being in his right wits and good judgments, turned away the fat knight with the great belly doublet." Fluellen admires Henry for rejecting Falstaff.

Comment

Fluellen is nowhere more comical and quaint than in this scene. His odd use of language includes repetition of hortatory phrases ("look you" and "mark you"), use of the singular for the plural form of the verb ("as my fingers is to my fingers"), and excessive redundancy (for example, referring to Alexander in "his rages and his furies, and his wraths, and his cholers, and his moods, and his displeasures, and his indignations"). Fluellen not only speaks quaintly. He is also not very logical. Because he greatly admires the ancient generals, he would like to think that Henry resembles Alexander the Great. Unfortunately, he can only think of the most absurdly irrelevant comparisons between the two men. Fluellen cannot remember the name of the river at Macedon, and even if he could, that would prove nothing: many, many towns have rivers. Fluellen approves of Henry's turning away Falstaff, but his comparison of this rejection with Alexander's murder of Cleitus does not establish any point of similarity between the two heroes.

Henry enters with several English lords and French prisoners. He declares that he was not angry since he came to France until this instant, and bids a herald ride to the French horsemen on the opposite hill and tell them either to come down and fight or yield the field. Otherwise, the English will come after them.

At this moment Montjoy appears to ask permission for the French to seek through the bloody battlefield to count and bury their dead. Henry says that he does not know whether the English have won, for French horsemen still gallop over the field. "The day is yours," Montjoy answers. Henry's next words are, "Praised be God and not our strength for it." Learning that the castle nearby is called Agincourt, Henry names this the field of Agincourt, fought on the day of Crispin Crispianus. Fluellen reminds the king that his ancestors Edward III and Edward the Black Prince fought brave battles in France and that Welshmen did very good service in those wars, wearing leeks in their caps. Henry says that he does not scorn to wear the leek in his cap on Saint Davy's day, "For I am Welsh, you know, good countryman." Fluellen declares that all the water in the Wye cannot wash out the king's Welsh blood from his veins. He says he is proud to be Henry's countryman. "I care not who know it. I will confess it to all the world. I need not to be ashamed of your majesty, praised be God, so long as your majesty is an honest man." Henry replies soberly, "God keep me so."

## Comment

Henry's immediate response to Montjoy's announcement of the English victory shows that his piety does not diminish with success. Before the battle he declared that the outcome was in God's hand, and now he attributes the victory to God rather than the strength of his men.

Fluellen is very proud that the king is a Welshman like himself, but he praises the king in a rather backhanded manner. Henry, however, does not mind Fluellen's bluntness. In fact, he rather appreciates the integrity of a man who does not know how to flatter.

Henry sends his heralds to go with Montjoy and bring him word of the French and English casualties. Then, noticing Williams, who has entered, he calls the soldier over and asks him why he wears a glove in his cap. Williams answers that the glove belongs to a man with whom he quarreled the previous night. If the stranger wears Williams's glove in his cap, the soldier promises to box his ear. Henry asks Fluellen if he thinks that Williams should keep his oath even if his adversary should turn out to be above his station. Fluellen replies that Williams is honor bound to fight the man, whoever he may be. Bidding the soldier keep his oath, Henry sends him off to fetch Gower. When he has left, the king asks Fluellen to wear a certain glove in his hat, which he says he got from the Duke of Alençon (while fighting him), but which really belongs to Williams. Henry tells Fluellen that anyone who challenges the glove must be a friend of Alençon's and an enemy of Henry's. The Welsh captain is honored to be allowed to show his devotion to the king by wearing the gage. Henry then sends Fluellen after Williams. When he has gone, the king explains the situation to Warwick and Gloucester, and asks them to follow Fluellen to see that no harm results from his encounter with Williams.

## Comment

Henry knows that Fluellen will meet Williams with Gower and he expects the soldier to challenge his glove. We will see in the next scene how Henry will manage to settle the dispute.

### SUMMARY

In scenes six and seven the following developments take place:

1. We learn that the Duke of York has died on the battlefield in the manner of a perfect chivalric hero. He typifies the ideal English warrior, true to the concepts of honor and loyalty.

2. As a result of the French rally, Henry orders all prisoners killed. This harsh decree wins the approval of Captain Gower, although we may find it unduly cruel. We must remember, however, that the French are equally cruel, for they have massacred the English boys.

3. Fluellen compares Henry to Alexander the Great in absurdly irrelevant ways. As usual Fluellen has the right idea in a general way, but his words are always

slightly ridiculous. As a result of his garbled speech, we may well wonder if there is any valid point of comparison between the two heroes, ancient and modern.

4. Montjoy tells Henry that the French concede that they are beaten. He asks and is granted permission for the French to seek through the bloody field for their dead and wounded.

5. Henry's reaction to victory shows his piety and modesty. He thanks God and not his own strength for the success.

6. Fluellen's bluntness extends even to his dealings with the king. He is a man who cannot flatter, no matter how great his admiration and devotion, and Henry appreciates this integrity of character.

7. Williams is called upon to explain to the king why he is wearing a glove in his cap. When he leaves, Henry asks Fluellen to wear the glove that belongs to Williams, but which Fluellen thinks was taken from an enemy of the king. He will see in the next scene what happens when Williams and Fluellen meet.

## ACT IV: SCENE 8

Fluellen encounters Gower and Williams returning to the king. Williams, noticing his glove in Fluellen's cap, strikes him and Fluellen seizes the soldier as a traitor to the king. Williams hotly denies the accusation, and the two men are scuffling when Warwick and Gloucester enter, followed closely by Henry himself. The king restores peace by revealing that he was the unidentified man of the previous night with whom Williams exchanged gages. He rebukes the soldier for the words he spoke in abuse of the king, but Williams replies with steadfast dignity, "Your majesty came not like yourself. You appeared to me but as a common man; witness the night, the garments, your lowliness. And what your highness suffered under that shape, I beseech you take it for your own fault, and not mine; for had you been as I took you for, I made no offense." The king is contented with this answer. He fills Williams' glove with money, and bids Fluellen make friends with the man. Impressed with the soldier's courage, Fluellen gives him a shilling (which Williams grudgingly accepts) and counsels him to avoid future quarrels.

## Comment

This incident may well strike us as rather peculiar. Why does Henry ask Fluellen to wear the gage that belongs to Williams, knowing that a fight will break out between the two quick-tempered men? We have already explained that the king was angered by Williams' skepticism regarding his promise not to be ransomed. He wants to frighten the soldier briefly and perhaps to test his courage when confronted by Fluellen, but he has no intention of punishing him. Williams shows himself to be honest and fearless and like Fluellen in his inability to gravel before authority. Rather than abjectly apologize for his words, he tells Henry what the king already knows: that there are words which one subject may speak to another that are unfitting for the king's ear. Henry knows that this is true, and he appreciates Williams' truthfulness just as he appreciated Fluellen's bluntness in the preceding scene. The comedy of this incident is tempered only by an underlying political truth. The king is a good fellow and he rewards the soldier, but the fact remains that his subjects can never speak to him as they do to one another.

An English herald returns with the list of casualties. He reports that the English have taken fifteen hundred French noblemen as prisoners (including Orleans and Bourbon), and a number of common soldiers as well. French dead number ten thousand, of whom one hundred and twenty-six are noblemen and eight thousand four hundred are lesser gentry. The French dead include the flower of the army: the Constable, Rambures, the Admiral of France, and several others whose impressive titles Henry reads aloud. The English losses are, by comparison, amazingly few: two noblemen (York and Suffolk), two gentry, and twenty-five others. Henry is moved and declares, "O God, thy arm was here! / And not to us, but to thy arm alone, Ascribe we all!" He orders that no man take the praise from God by boasting of this victory. When Fluellen asks wistfully if they may tell the number of men killed, the king consents on condition that divine aid be acknowledged at all times. Henry commands that religious services be sung and the dead buried. Then the army will set out for Calais and for England, "Where ne'er from France arrived more happy men."

## Comment

Historians disagree as to the exact number of English and French losses, but all agree that the disparity was enormous. The best estimate is that the French lost about ten thousand and the English about four hundred men. This extraordinary victory is explained by historians in terms of strategy and arms, something which Shakespeare never mentions. The French army relied on heavily armored cavalry, who were no match for the lightly armored and consequently more mobile English archers.

The French were further hampered by a muddy field in which their horses foundered, delaying their advance. All this is made clear in Holinshed's chronicle, but Shakespeare chose to speak only about the difference in spirit between the English and the French. Henry attributes the victory entirely to God with a modesty and piety becoming a Christian king. Shakespeare thus makes the outcome seem more miraculous than it really was.

**SUMMARY**

This scene is important for the following reasons:

1. The quarrel between the king and Williams is resolved with good feeling restored on both sides. Although the incident is amusing, neither Henry nor the soldier loses his dignity.

2. The casualties of both sides are revealed, and we learn that the French army has been decimated by the seemingly inferior English forces.

3. Henry attributes the English success to God's help and forbids his army to boast of their prowess.

4. We learn that the English will return home as soon as possible.

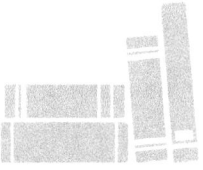

# HENRY V

## TEXTUAL ANALYSIS

## ACT 5

### ACT V: SCENE 1

The Chorus once again fills us in on the events not presented on stage. We must imagine the king's arrival at Calais and embarkation for England, where an ecstatic throng of men, women and children awaits him at Southampton. His lords want to have his injured sword and helmet displayed along the road to London, but Henry refuses to permit such ostentation. "Being free from vainness and self-glorious pride," he gives all honor to God and disclaims any for himself. His arrival in London is as triumphal as Caesar's return to Rome. The mayor and all the citizens turn out to greet him, as they would greet the English general were he to return now from Ireland. (In 1599, at the time Shakespeare was writing Henry V, Lord Essex was in Ireland, quelling a rebellion against the queen.) Henry remains in London until an emissary comes on behalf of France to try to arrange peace terms. Then the king crosses the Channel and we must follow him back to France.

## Comment

The reference to the Irish rebellion reminds us that Elizabeth was faced with the problem of maintaining national unity. Shakespeare represents Henry as having achieved the loyalty of all parts of his realm, something for which the Tudor queen was still striving.

The battle of Agincourt was fought on October 24, 1415. The Treaty of Troyes, establishing peace between England and France, was signed in 1420. Shakespeare jumps over the intervening five years, ignoring the second French campaign waged by Henry during that time.

It is one day after Saint Davy's day. Gower asks Fluellen why he is still wearing a leek in his hat, and Fluellen explains that on the previous day Pistol impudently brought him bread and salt and ordered him to eat his leek. At that time and in that place a fight was out of the question, but Fluellen intends to wear the leek until he meets the cowardly braggart again. At this moment Pistol enters "swelling like a turkey cock," and Fluellen, ignoring Pistol's protests that he hates the taste and smell of leek, forces him to eat every morsel of the vegetable. As "sauce" for the leek and by way of encouragement to the reluctant Pistol, the Welshman rains blows upon him. When he has finished, Fluellen compels him to accept a groad (a small coin), threatening to make him eat another leek if he refuses to accept the money. Warning the rascal to keep out of his way, Fluellen exits.

Once his enemy is safely out of earshot, Pistol boldly threatens revenge, declaring that "All hell shall stir for this." Gower reproves the "counterfeit cowardly knave" for mocking an ancient and honorable Welsh tradition. Fluellen's Welsh manner of speech diminishes neither his valor nor his skill with a good English cudgel, as Pistol has learned by experience.

Gower exits and Pistol, left alone on the stage, ruminates that Fortune has turned against him. He has received news that his wife is dead. Suddenly he feels old and weary. But he still has thoughts for the future. He decides to become a bawd and a cutpurse. "To England will I steal, and there I'll steal; / And patches will I get unto these cudgelled scars / And swear I got them in the Gallia wars."

## Comment

In many respects Pistol fits the stock type of braggart soldier descended from the Roman Plautus. . . . In the third act (scene six) we saw that Pistol was angry at Fluellen for refusing to intercede on behalf of Bardolph. In the fourth act (scene one) Pistol boasted to the king that he would make Fluellen eat his leek on Saint Davy's day, and now we learn that he tried to do so. It is just like the cowardly Pistol to have carried out his threat by taunting the Welshman in a place where the latter could not offer to fight him for the insult. But Fluellen is not a man to forget an affront, especially if it involves his honor as a Welshman.

This is the last scene of the comic subplot in the play, and like the others it depends for humor largely on the speech peculiarities of Pistol and Fluellen. We feel a certain satisfaction that Pistol, after his unwarranted contemptuous behavior towards Fluellen, has been forced to eat the leek. He has only forgotten what was coming to him. It comes as no surprise that Pistol plans to turn rogue in England. We know that Bardolph and Nym have already died on the gallows for theft. Now we learn that there is a good likelihood that Pistol will end up the same way. The amiable rogues of Henry IV have all come to a bad end.

### SUMMARY

In this scene the following developments take place:

1. The Chorus tells us that Henry has returned in triumph to England, where he remains until the French sue for peace. Shakespeare deliberately jumps over the five years intervening between Agincourt and the Treaty of Troyes. We are prepared to see the king next in France.

2. The quarrel between Fluellen and Pistol is finally resolved in this last comic scene of the play. The Welshman punishes Pistol for his disrespect by forcing him to eat the very leek that he threatened to make Fluellen eat. Pistol is every bit the coward we always knew him to be.

3. Pistol expresses his intention of becoming a rogue and thief in England. We can have no doubt that he will live up to his word.

## ACT V: SCENE 2

The scene takes place in the French court. Henry and his chief lords (Exeter, Bedford, Warwick, and others) enter from one side, while the French king, queen, princess, the Duke of Burgundy, and others enter from the other side. Henry's first words immediately reveal the purpose of this assembly, "Peace to this meeting, wherefore we are met!" He wishes health and joy to his "brother" and "sister," the French king and queen, and to his "most fair and princely cousin," Katherine. Turning to Burgundy and all the French peers, he salutes them with royal dignity. The French king welcomes Henry and the English princes in equally formal but briefer terms. "Right joyous are we to behold your face." The queen expresses her hope for a happy settlement of the present griefs and quarrels.

The Duke of Burgundy is intermediary between England and France. (At that time Burgundy was an independent land, and its duke at least as powerful as the king of France.) He has done his best to bring the two parties together, and now he asks what hindrance can there be to restoring peace to France. In a lengthy speech he tells how the "naked, poor, and mangled Peace" was driven from fertile France, where ruin and desolation ensued. Gardens, vineyards, and meadows, once carefully tended, are neglected and grow wild. Moreover, he adds, the French children, like the gardens, run wild, for all their experience is of bloody and fearful deeds. In conclusion, he asks the princes here assembled to restore the natural harmony and order to this "best garden of the world" that is France.

Henry replies that the French may buy the precious gifts of peace by acceding to the English demands. The French king requests a conference with Henry's counselors so that he may deliberate and pronounce his final answer on the spot. Henry appoints his uncle Exeter, his brothers Clarence and Gloucester, and two other lords to negotiate the peace terms with the French. The queen declares her intention of attending the conference in the hope that a woman's voice may prove soothing to stubborn men. Henry asks that Katherine be left with him, since she is first among his demands. The queen agrees and all exit except Henry, Katherine, and Alice.

## Comment

This part of the scene is marked by ceremonial formality. The monarchs address each other in the official terms of amity, "Brother England" and "Brother France." The queen seems somewhat more relaxed and natural. She hopes that her feminine persuasiveness may influence the negotiators, just as Katherine may soften Henry's demands. Burgundy's presence adds to the pomp and ceremony of the scene. He serves still another important function. As a neutral party with strong personal feelings for the French land (to which his duchy is near neighbor), he can talk about the blessings of peace and the ravages of war without compromising his position. The French king would not deliver such remarks in public for fear of undermining his bargaining position. Likewise Henry, the victor, would not discourse to his vanquished enemy on the advantages of peace. That would be insolent and out of place. Therefore, assuming that Shakespeare wanted someone in this scene to remind us that peace is an extremely desirable goal, we feel that this speech could only be uttered by a disinterested sovereign such as Burgundy.

Left to woo Katherine (chaperoned by Alice), Henry does so with the high spirits of a plain-talking soldier. He starts by asking her to teach him the soft terms that will move a lady's heart. For he is unused to the gentle ways of court society. Katherine thinks he must be mocking her, since she cannot speak English well, but Henry answers that he will be happy to hear her declare her love in broken English. When he asks "do you like me?" she answers that she does not know what is "like me," and Henry, punning, tells her that an angel is like her. Katherine understands his words, declaring, in French, that men are full of deceits. As if in answer to her charge. Henry vows that he can woo only in plain and simple speech. As if addressing a comrade in arms, he asks her to consent and shake hands on the bargain. He has neither verses nor dances to win a lady's favor, but if fighting, or leaping on his horse could win her approval, he would quickly win a wife. "But before God, Kate, I cannot look greenly nor grasp out my eloquence, nor I have no cunning in protestation, only downright oaths which I never use till urged, nor never break for urging." If she will have him, good. If she refuse, he will not die of grief, and yet he loves her. He advises her that he is sure to be constant in his affection. Lacking the ability to win the favors of other ladies, he cannot then be false to her. "A good leg will fall, a straight back will stoop, a black beard will turn white, a curled pate will grow bald," he tells her, "but a good heart, Kate, is the sun and the moon." Therefore, he urges, "If thou would have such a one, take me; and take me, take a soldier; take a soldier, take a king."

Katherine asks if it is possible that she should love the enemy of France. He answers that he is not the enemy but the friend of France, for he loves France so well that he will not part with a single village. And, he adds. "When France is mine and I am yours, then yours is France and you are mine." Because she cannot follow this in English, he repeats it in halting French. Becoming more confident, he tells her that he knows she loves him, and at night, with Alice, will dispraise those parts she likes best in him. He asks her to be merciful, "because I love thee cruelly." Still more jovial, he tells her that between them they will produce a boy, half-English and half-French, who will defeat the Turks.

Reverting briefly to the traditional language of the wooer, he calls her, in French, "the most beautiful Katherine in the world" and "my dearest and divine goddess." She declares that his false French could deceive the wisest maiden in France, but Henry, unabashed, continues both to dispraise his own ability as a lover and to swear his love for her. Finally he demands outright. "Wilt thou have me?" She replies that she will have him if it pleases the king, her father. Henry declares that it certainly shall please the king, and Katherine says that then it shall also content her. Upon these words Henry calls her his queen and silences her objection that it is not the custom in France for girls to kiss before they are married by telling her that customs are made by kings and therefore may be broken by kings. Kissing her, he declares. "You have witchcraft in your lips, Kate." One kiss from her, he says, would have more effect on him than the French Council or a petition of monarchs.

## Comment

Most of the scene is in English, but some French is spoken. We see that Katherine has achieved a fairly good understanding of English, and Henry can speak a little French. The two manage to understand one another despite the slight language barrier.

Henry rejects the **conventions** of romantic love in his wooing of the princess. He simply refuses to utter the stereotyped platitudes of a heart-sick lover who swears that he will die in grief if the lady refuses. He dispraises his own exterior, but promises that his heart (what really matters) will be true to her.

It is interesting to note that he speaks to her in prose, declaring that he has "neither words nor measure" for verses. In the orations to his soldiers and, in fact, in all his encounters with men of noble rank, Henry speaks in perfect if not eloquent verse. The prose in this scene is designed to emphasize the simplicity, honesty, and bluntness of his manner of wooing.

Henry says that he loves Katherine, but he also remarks that he loves France so well that he will not part with a single village. There is no doubt that this is a political marriage. He is determined to be king of France. And yet, it would be wrong to think that Henry is not charmed by Katherine. She was known to be a beautiful and charming girl, and she has spirit enough to let Henry know that she is not taken in by flattery when he calls her "angel" or "goddess." If we object that Henry has had no chance to know her and therefore cannot really love her, we are failing to understand this scene in the way that an Elizabethan audience would have done. Love at first sight is a standard romantic stage **convention**. Moreover, most marriages at that time were arranged on the basis of economic or political considerations, and the couple was expected to grow to love one another after they were man and wife. Henry is probably delighted that the girl whom it is expedient for him to marry is also extremely charming.

The French and English lords return. Henry and Burgundy exchange slightly bawdy remarks about the progress of the wooing. The jokes turn mainly on the fact that Cupid, the god of love, is traditionally represented as a naked and blind boy, whom a sheltered maiden would be embarrassed to look upon. Finally Henry says that the French may be thankful that his love for Katherine has made him blind to many French cities. He is told that the French king has agreed to all the English demands, including Katherine, except for the form of address which he will use in writing to his son-in-law. Henry has insisted upon being addressed in French and in Latin "Our very dear son Henry, king of England, inheritor of France." The French king readily concedes this point now. He bids Henry take his daughter, and with her raise a son who will unite the two countries, planting peace "In their fair bosoms, that never war advance / His bleeding sword t'wixt England and fair France." To this all present cry amen, and Henry kisses Katherine as his queen. The French queen invokes the blessing of God on the couple, that their two hearts and two realms may be united and Englishmen and Frenchmen may be as brothers. Again all cry amen. Henry orders that preparations be made for the wedding, on which day he will ask Burgundy and all the peers to guarantee the peace terms. "Then shall I swear to Kate, and you to me, / And may our oaths well kept and prosp'rous be!" All exit.

## Comment

Historical sources tell us that Katherine was in fact very beautiful and that on her account Henry did consent to mitigate slightly his demands. Thus his remark that he cannot see "many a fair French city for one fair French maid that stands in my way" has some basis in fact. The form of address that Henry wants the French king to use is significant for the words "inheritor of France." He wants it to be absolutely clear that he will inherit the French crown from the present king. Because Latin was then the lingua franca of Europe and the language of diplomacy, the terms are repeated in Latin as well as French. Asking disinterested parties to commit themselves to the upholding of a peace agreement was not unusual in the fifteenth century, nor for that matter is it uncommon nowadays. Henry intends to make Burgundy and the French peers swear to take sides against the aggressor if the peace is broken unilaterally.

The Chorus returns to deliver an epilogue. For the last time he apologizes for the "rough and all unable pen" of the author, and for the temerity of trying to represent the glory of such great historical personnages. He concludes by reminding us that though Henry left his infant son lord of England and of France, in the reign of that son (Henry VI) France was lost and England witnessed the beginning of a long and bloody civil strife.

## Comment

The final scene concludes in an atmosphere of general optimism and joy. It was a **convention** of comedy that the play should end with a marriage. *Henry V* is the only one of Shakespeare's history plays to end in this way, just as it is the only history play to celebrate a heroic king rather than to describe a monarch with a fatal weakness. At the conclusion of this play we see the hero at the apex of his glory. He has been victorious in war, in diplomacy, and in love. Peace at home is augmented by victory abroad, and Henry promises to have a son who will continue in his footsteps. But the comic spirit is undercut at the very end. It is left to the Chorus to remind us of the facts of history. For many long years after the death of Henry. England did not see his like again. Shakespeare's audience could not help but see a parallel for that "Star of England" in their own Queen Elizabeth.

### SUMMARY

This last scene concludes the action in the following ways:

1. Henry has returned to France to negotiate a peace treaty. The two parties meet with great dignity and formality to conclude the final agreement. This was an ideal opportunity to display pomp and ceremony on stage.

2. The Duke of Burgundy tells of the ravages the war has made in France, and we became aware that beneath the glory and honor of warfare is destruction and grief.

3. The friendly and jocular tone that Henry takes with Katherine is in marked contrast to the heavy formality of his dealings with her father and the court. Henry acts the plain soldier wooing a lady in frank and pleasant terms. He is gay and persuasive, but we feel an underlying seriousness to his words. If he does not love Katherine in the sense that we use the word love, he is certainly very anxious to marry her for other reasons. The few words that Katherine speaks show her to be a girl of spirit and fully aware that the decision rests with her father rather than herself.

4. The French king agrees to all Henry's demands, including Katherine, and promises that Henry will inherit the French throne.

5. The scene concludes with general optimism about the future harmony between England and France. Henry looks forward to having a son who will fulfill the hopes of both countries.

6. In an epilogue, the Chorus returns to remind us that the future did not turn out as happy as Henry and his followers hoped. In the reign of Henry VI, England lost possession of France and the Wars of the Roses began in England.

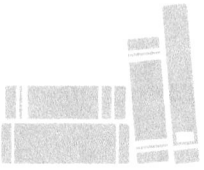

# HENRY V

## CHARACTER ANALYSES

### HENRY PLANTAGENET, KING HENRY V

The subject as well as the main character of the play. He is on stage a good deal of the time, and even when he is not present, he is still a significant factor in the action of others. The scenes in the French court are directly related to the character and actions of King Henry. The comic scenes are equally bound up with the character of the king. Thus, Falstaff has to die because his presence is inimical to the concept of a hero-king, and Pistol, Bardolph and Nym all come to a bad end after flouting the principles for which the king stands.

While he was a prince, Henry led a wild and merry life among the lower elements of society. After becoming king, he underwent what appears to the Archbishop to be a miraculous conversion. In the play Henry IV Part I, Shakespeare showed that Prince Hal knew what he was doing all along, firmly intending to change his ways when the time came for him to be king. In *Henry V*, although no rational explanation is offered for the startling change in his behavior, there is a fairly clear implication that the quality of kingship in Henry was always constant.

Throughout the play Henry is presented as the ideal king. Even before he appears in person, the churchmen declare their unbounded admiration for him, and in the course of the play their judgment is confirmed. Henry is undoubtedly a man endowed with political genius. In *Henry IV* Part II, his father, on his death bed, advised him to undertake foreign wars in order to prevent dissension at home. Henry has taken this counsel to heart, but he has also seen the advantage of soliciting the advice and approval of the most important men of the kingdom. Thus he places the highly influential Archbishop of Canterbury in the position of accepting responsibility for the war by confirming Henry's legal and moral right to the French crown. Furthermore, the king makes sure of the support of the nobility before he commits himself. Finally, Henry prudently considers the possibility of a Scottish invasion while he is away. It is only when he is sure of the wisdom of the venture that he decides to go to war.

Henry is an outstanding general both in his understanding of military tactics and in his ability to win the confidence and enthusiastic approval of his soldiers. He never betrays any personal fear; he himself fights in the forefront of the army, and he refuses to save himself by ransom. If the army is defeated he will die with his men. His brilliant speeches at the gates of Harfleur and before Agincourt are effective in raising the morale of his soldiers.

Henry's piety is remarkable throughout the play. He affirms an absolute reliance on God to determine the outcome of the war, and when victory is won, he thanks God and not his own power for it.

On the whole Henry gives the impression of a man exceptionally well-suited to the role of the king, yet there are times when the burdens of high office are particularly oppressive.

When his friends turn traitor against him he becomes keenly aware that, as king, he can never fully trust the men around him. Again, the night before the battle of Agincourt, he realizes that, unlike other men, he cannot confess his fear and express the feelings common to all mortal men in time of danger. The privacy of ordinary men is something that he can never enjoy, and he can never relax his vigil for the national welfare.

Although as a king Henry is far more sober and serious than he was as a prince, he likes to think of himself as a hearty good fellow as well as a regal monarch. His practical joke on Williams shows, that he has not completely lost his sense of humor and of fun. In the presence of the French king and court Henry is properly dignified, but alone with Katherine he reveals another side of his character: unsophisticated simplicity, bluntness, and good humor.

Henry is essentially a man of action, and that is why he is such a successful king. Yet he is not completely free from moral conflicts. Thus, in several speeches he reveals an awareness of and concern for the suffering that will inevitably attend his war against France. In the first act he calls himself a "Christian king," and in his speech to the conspirators and to the Governor of Harfleur he expresses feelings of pity and a natural inclination to mercy. In order to be a great and glorious king, however, he must and does suppress his moral scruples. That is why in the first act he makes the Archbishop accept the moral responsibility for the war, and in the second act makes the Governor of Hartfleur seem responsible for the slaughter of his people if the town does not surrender. Henry is constantly absolving himself of guilt for the victims of the war, because his chief concern is not moral but practical and political. For Henry the most important thing about the conflict with France is that it is an opportunity to win glory and honor for himself and for England. These considerations ultimately carry greater weight with him than anything else.

## THE DUKE OF EXETER

Henry's uncle and chief advisor. The king solicits his opinion on the question of war with France and then sends him as special messenger to the court across the Channel. When Harfleur surrenders, Exeter is given charge of the city, but instead of remaining there he joins the main body of the army before Agincourt. Fluellen calls him a brave gentleman, and Fluellen does not dispense praise without cause. During the peace negotiations Exeter is chief among the English counselors. A soldier and a statesman, he is brave, loyal, and completely trustworthy.

## THE DUKE OF YORK

Second cousin to Henry and an older man. He begs for and receives the most dangerous position in the battle, leading the foremost troops. An ideal knight in death as in life, he dies in battle murmuring words of friendship for the dead Earl of Suffolk and loyalty to the king.

## THE EARL OF WESTMORELAND

Another of the king's advisors who urges him to make war on France. Shakespeare includes him among the noble present at the battle of Agincourt, although historically he was not there. It is he who, wishing for additional English troops, prompts Henry's famous Crispin Crispianus speech.

## THE DUKE OF BEDFORD

Brother of the king, appears briefly in the scene before the battle of Agincourt, where his few lines show him to be honorable and courageous. Historically, Bedford was in England at this time.

## THE DUKE OF GLOUCESTER

Henry's youngest brother, seems to have a responsible position in the army, for he is mentioned as being in charge of the mines at Harfleur, but he is less confident than Henry before the battle of Agincourt. At the end of the third act Henry reproves him for hoping that the French will not insist upon a battle, and in the first scene of the fourth act Henry again cheers his brother with optimistic words. In the concluding scene of the play, Gloucester is one of several nobles who negotiate peace terms with the French king.

## THE DUKE OF CLARENCE AND THE EARLS OF WARWICK AND SALISBURY

Appear in the entourage of the king but neither say nor do anything of note.

## THE ARCHBISHOP OF CANTERBURY

The highest ecclesiastical figure in England, is chiefly concerned with preserving the church lands, although he feels a genuine admiration for the king and loyalty to his country. His speech to the king about Salique law is intricate and boring, but his speech, about division of labor and responsibility among the bees is a fine **exposition** of the Elizabethan ideal of order and degree in society. He appears in the two scenes of the first act and is never mentioned again.

## THE BISHOP OF ELY

Shares the interests and attitudes of Canterbury, whose argument he supports before the king.

## THE THREE CONSPIRATORS

The make only a token appearance on stage. Except for their urging Henry not to show clemency to a man in prison for slandering him, they in no way reveal why they were moved to betray their king. Lord Scroop is a particularly close friend of Henry's and a man whom the king especially admired as a religious, scholarly, and uncorrupted individual. That is why the king is deeply distressed by his betrayal. The Earl Of Cambridge denies that he was corrupted by money, but he does not explain what his real motive was (historically, Cambridge hoped that his relative Edmund Mortimer would become king). Sir Thomas Grey was also a friend of Henry's and, like the others, he offers no justification for his action. When the three men learn that they have been discovered and hear Henry's moving words about loyalty to king and country, they all rejoice that their plot has been prevented and beg forgiveness for their sins (but not for their bodies) as they are led off to execution.

## SIR THOMAS ERPINGHAM

A gentleman who commands part of Henry's army. He is no longer young, but he bears the hardships of the campaign with cheerful good humor. He is clearly devoted to the king and is much respected by the soldiers.

## FLUELLEN

A Welsh captain in Henry's army, is one of the most original comic characters in all Shakespeare. Henry sums up his characters in Act IV, Scene I when he says, "Though it appear a little out of fashion, / There is much care and valor in this Welshman." He is very much out of fashion; that is, he is quaint and comical. But he is also a brave and loyal soldier, a man who says what he thinks and is incapable of guile and flattery.

Like many other comic characters, Fluellen has certain speech peculiarities (for example, saying "p" for "b"), but these are generally related to his Welsh origin. He loves to hear himself talk and to expound on certain favorite subjects, especially ancient warfare. Pedantic and conceited, he thinks he knows all about a subject of which he is actually ignorant. His knowledge about Alexander the Great and Pompey is both limited and erroneous. Moreover, Fluellen's logic is something that he alone can follow. No one else would find his reasoning a convincing intellectual exercise.

Finally, Fluellen is quick-tempered and always ready to pick a fight. He is jealous of Macmorris, the Irish captain, and wants to fight him on the grounds that he underestimates the importance of the ancient rules of warfare. He is delighted to punish Pistol for his insolence. And when the king asks him to wear a gage for him, he is greatly pleased and honored.

### Gower

An English captain, more ordinary and therefore less interesting than his friend Fluellen. Gower seems to know more than Fluellen does (for example, the name of the town where Alexander the Great was born), but he does not exhibit his knowledge unless actually called upon. He is quieter than Fluellen but he is a reliable judge of character, for he recognizes Pistol as a scoundrel as soon as he sees him, and foresees the kind of end he will come to. Gower is dramatically a foil for Fluellen's peculiarities.

### MACMORRIS

An Irish captain who is in charge of the mines that the Duke of Gloucester is constructing in front of Harfleur. Fluellen, probably jealous of him, picks a quarrel with Macmorris, who is not as concerned with the question of the ancient disciplines of war as Fluellen thinks he should be. Macmorris is impatient at standing around and talking when there is fighting to be done. He is interested in action more than debate, and luckily a parley interrupts the impending conflict between the two men. Macmorris' speech indicates his Irish origins, a subject on which he is rather touchy.

### JAMY

A Scots captain, speaks in the Scots manner. Fluellen likes him because he is an admirer of the ancient disciplines of war and also probably because he prefers to listen to others debate than to argue himself.

## ALEXANDER COURT, JOHN BATES, AND MICHAEL WILLIAMS

Three common soldiers in Henry's army, with whom the king, disguised, talks on the eve of battle. Alexander Court speaks only once to remark that dawn is breaking. John Bates is apprehensive about the coming day and thinks that the king must be equally afraid even if he does not show his fear. Bates believes that a subject has no right to question the king's cause. He is resolved to fight lustily for the king without seeking to judge the merits of the quarrel. If the king be in the wrong, then the king alone bears the guilt for the sins his subjects commit in fighting in his cause.

## MICHAEL WILLIAMS

The most interesting and complicated of the soldiers. He ponders the question of the king's responsibility for the death of his men in battle, but finally concedes Henry's contention that every man is responsible for his own soul. Williams is sceptical about the king's promise not to be ransomed, and as a result Henry quarrels with him. They exchange gages in order to recognize and fight each other, but after the battle the king gives his gage to Fluellen. Before the two men can fight in earnest, Henry reveals his identity of the night before and Williams replies with dignity that the king must not blame him for words which were not meant as an insult. The king is responsible, since he appeared in disguise. Henry concedes this to be true. Williams represents an ideal of English manhood, for he stands up for his own innocence and dignity even before the king, and Henry admires him for this.

## BARDOLPH

His red nose and carbuncled cheeks are familiar to Shakespeare's audiences from *Henry IV,* where he was one of Prince Hal's roistering companions. In *Henry V,* however, his cowardice and thievery are less amusing than they were in the earlier play. He urges Pistol and Nym to resolve their quarrel in order that the three of them can profit from the expedition against France. He is not in the least moved by the thought of a war for England's honor or his own. Before the battle of Agincourt Bardolph is caught stealing from a church and is hanged. His death is as inglorious as his life.

## PISTOL

Also familiar from the earlier history plays as a rogue and a thief, has married Mistress Quickly and is as jealous of his wife as of his money. Pistol, a variation of the stock figure of the braggart soldier, is by far the funniest of the comic low characters because of his ridiculously bombastic and high-flown language. Because he is a coward, he does not dare to fight Nym. Instead he threatens him with fierce but funny words declaimed in a stream of **blank verse**. Finally Pistol and Nym make up because they find it most expedient to do so.

Pistol's quarrel with Fluellen originates when the Welshman refuses to intercede with the authorities on behalf of Bardolph, who has been caught stealing. Pistol's mock fierceness enables him to capture one poor scared French prisoner, but his basic cowardice comes out when Fluellen finally gives him a well-deserved drubbing. Pistol's mockery of the Welsh custom of wearing the leek on Saint Davy's day shows that he has no respect for an honorable tradition. There is no doubt that Pistol will come to as grievous an end as his companions, for he decides to return to England, pretending to be a wounded veteran while really a thief.

## NYM

A comic character in *The Merry Wives of Windsor* as well as *Henry V,* is as much of a knave and a coward as Pistol is, but his temperament is melancholy rather than choleric, and he is given to uttering enigmatically pessimistic remarks. Like Bardolph he dies on the gallows as a thief.

## THE BOY

He was in the service of Falstaff. When the knight dies, the Boy enters into the employment of the three rogues bound for France. Although he is their servant, he is morally their superior, for he refuses to steal as they would have him do. Before he has a chance to seek another position, he is killed with the other lackeys during the battle of Agincourt.

## THE HOSTESS, MISTRESS QUICKLY

She was the tavernkeeper in *Henry IV.* Now she is married to Pistol, whom she loves well it seems. She is genuinely concerned over Falstaff's illness, and her account of his death is wonderfully moving. Of all the comic characters she is the only one who shows warmth and a loving disposition.

## FALSTAFF

The marvelous comic figure of *Henry IV* parts I and II, does not appear in person, as Shakespeare promised he would in the end of *Henry IV,* Part II. Instead we are told first that he is very ill and then that he has died. It seems likely that Shakespeare cut him from the play either because the actor who usually played his part (Will Kempe) left the repertory company that year, or because Falstaff's contempt for authority is incompatible with the rest of the play, which glorifies the strong monarchy of *Henry V.*

## THE FRENCH KING

During the reign of Henry V, this was Charles VI, a weak ruler who for long periods of time was actually insane. Shakespeare does depict his as utterly without dignity, however, for in comparison with his son he is relatively mature and prudent in his judgments. Thus he recognizes the seriousness of the English threat and insists on adequate preparations to meet the invasion. He is much older than Henry, and probably partly because of his age, he does not personally take part in the fighting. His son does not obey him (refusing to remain at Rouen during the battle of Agincourt), but the other courtiers are suitably deferential to the king.

## THE DAUPHIN

Heir apparent to the French throne, is a childish, petulant, rude, and irresponsible young man. He shows lack of judgment in his ill-mannered jest of the tennis balls (historically accurate) and in his refusal to acknowledge that Henry is no longer a frivolous prince but a serious monarch, despite the first-hand reports of his ambassadors. The Dauphin, like Pistol, talks rather than acts. He indulges in absurd praise of his horse and brags about his own prowess, but his comrades (particularly the Constable) are contemptuous of his intelligence and his courage. During the battle, when the tide turns against the French, the Dauphin expresses his determination to rally his men, but his name is not among the wounded or the prisoners. Historically, the Dauphin was not presents at the battle of Agincourt. Actually there were three dauphins between 1415 and 1420, but Shakespeare only depicts the first of the three, who died soon after Agincourt. He is not present in the final scene in which peace is established, since by that time this dauphin was dead.

## THE CONSTABLE OF FRANCE

Commander-in-chief of the army, is a more impressive figure than the Dauphin, for he at least is willing to take Henry seriously. He seems genuinely concerned for the honor of France and is ready to lay down his life in battle. Although his ready wit does not spare the weaknesses of the Dauphin's character, the Constable does not himself possess the qualities of leadership that distinguish King Henry. He is never seen among his soldiers as Henry is, nor, in fact, in any serious contemplation of the war. He is killed in battle.

## THE DUKE OF ORLEANS

He defends his cousin, the Dauphin, against the Constable's slighting remarks. Otherwise he is perfectly undistinguished.

## THE DUKE OF BRITAINE

A very powerful lord, speaks only once and that is in the fifth scene of the third act to express his shame that the English have been permitted to advance so far into French territory, and to declare his eagerness to fight this contemptible enemy.

## THE DUKE OF BERRI

Another member of the French court who does not distinguish himself in any way except to insist that the English are beneath contempt and to rush into the fray, confident of success.

## RAMBURES AND GRANDPRE

Slightly less important commanders in the army. Each of the two makes a few disparaging remarks about the English and threats of French retaliation against the audacious enemy. It is later learned that Grandpre was killed in action.

## MONTJOY

The French herald, represents his master the king on errands to Henry. He comes twice to bid the English king consider what ransom he will offer, and he bears Henry's message of defiance back. The third time he appears his bearing is more humble, for he comes to ask permission for the French to seek through the field of their dead. Montjoy does his office well, and after his first visit Henry rewards him with a purse.

## THE FRENCH QUEEN, ISABELLE

She appears only in the final scene where, gracious and regal, she pleads for reconciliation and peace. Aware that a woman's voice may have a softening influence, she joins the peace conference, thereby cleverly leaving Henry alone with Katherine.

## PRINCESS KATHERINE

She is well aware that her destiny in life is to marry the man her father chooses on the basis of political necessity. In her first scene she is an apt pupil of English. In her second scene, listening to Henry's suit, she shows that she has made good progress in her language lessons and, moreover, that she is a girl of some spirit, for she chides the king for deceit on the two occasions that he flatters her in the language of courtship. She is as realistic as he is about the political aspect of their marriage, but she is less ready to defy **convention** by kissing before betrothal. Henry is apparently pleased with her beauty and charm as well as her dowry.

This Katherine, who married Henry, survived him and later married Owen Tudor, an ancestor of Queen Elizabeth and the Tudor dynasty. She was therefore, a particularly interesting personality in the mind of Shakespeare's audience.

## ALICE

The princess' maid and companion, is funny as an English teacher who thinks that her command of the language is far better than it really is. During the courting scene she remains discreetly in the background, interposing only when necessary to translate.

## THE DUKE OF BURGUNDY

An independent ruler the equal of the kings of England and France, appears only in the final scene in connection with the Treaty of Troyes as a mediator between the opposing parties. He jokes with Henry in rather bawdy terms, but he is also serious about the importance of restoring peace. His remarks about the evils of war and the benefits of peace is an effective counterpart to the glorification of war implicit in scenes such as Act IV Scene I (Henry Crispin Crispianus Day speech).

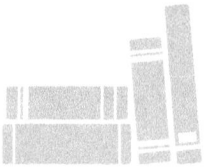

# HENRY V

## CRITICAL COMMENTARY

### SUMMARY OF CRITICAL COMMENTARY

Over the years critics have disagreed considerably over the interpretation and evaluation of *Henry V.* Essentially, the critics can be divided into those who admire the play and appreciate Henry as the ideal king, and those who are disgusted, or merely bored, by Henry and think poorly of the play as a whole. In between these extremes of judgment there are various shades of more moderate opinion.

### EARLY CRITICISM

One of the earliest commentators on the play was the eighteenth-century scholar, Dr. Samuel Johnson. He thought the play was interesting and well constructed and its hero thoroughly admirable up until the fifth act when, according to Johnson, Shakespeare ran out of material, and allowed his **protagonist** to degenerate into a mere good-natured fellow of a very ordinary sort. "I know no reason," wrote Dr. Johnson, "why Shakespeare now gives the king nearly such a character as he made him formerly ridicule in Percy (Hotspur). This military grossness and unskillfulness in all the softer arts does not suit very well with the gaieties of his youth, with the general knowledge ascribed to him at his accession, nor with the contemptuous message sent him by the Dauphin, who represents him as fitter for the ball room than the field, and tells him that he is not to 'revel into dutchies,' or win provinces 'with a nimble galliard'."

## THE ROMANTIC VIEW

In 1817 the essayist and critic William Hazlitt, who shared the republican sentiment of his friends, the Romantic poets Byron and Shelley, attacked *Henry V* as a glorification of principles most repugnant to nineteenth-century radicals: absolute monarchy, feudalism, and militarism. About the character of the king he wrote, "He was a hero - that is, he was ready to sacrifice his own life for the pleasure of destroying thousands of other lives. . . . How do we like him? We like him in the play. There he is a very amiable monster, a very splendid pageant. As we like to gaze at a panther or a young lion in their cages in the Tower and catch a pleasing horror from their glistening eyes, their velvet paws and dreadless roar, so we take a very romantic, heroic, patriotic and poetical delight in the boasts and feats of our younger Harry as they appear on the stage and are confined to lines of ten syllables." Hazlitt felt that Shakespeare intended Henry to be a hero, but that in fact the king turned out to be an extremely unattractive personality, despotic and cruel.

## MODERN CRITICS ANTAGONISTIC TO HENRY V

Mark Van Doren, twentieth-century poet and scholar, is also unalterably hostile to the play and its central character, but for different reasons. Van Doren feels that by the time he was writing this last of his historic plays, Shakespeare was dissatisfied with the simple man of action as his hero, and that the author's boredom with his subject communicates itself to the audience. Van Doren contends that Shakespeare was already looking forward to creating his complex tragic characters such as Hamlet and Macbeth. This is his explanation for the abrupt change in Henry's character in the fifth act, which Van Doren, like Dr. Johnson, considers a salient weakness of the play. "The figure whom he has groomed to be the ideal English king, all plumes and smiles and decorated courage, collapses here into a mere good fellow, a hearty undergraduate with enormous initials on his chest. The reason must be that Shakespeare has little interest in the ideal English king." Van Doren also criticizes the play on the grounds that much of its poetry is comparatively banal, and that the use of the Chorus indicates an uneasiness on the part of the author.

A few important early twentieth-century poets have also taken a dim view of the play. John Masefield wrote that "Henry V is the one commonplace man in the eight (history) plays.... He has the knack of life that fits human beings for whatever is animal in human affairs." William Butler Yeats commented on Henry: "He has the gross vices, the coarse nerves, of one who is to rule among violent people.... He is as remorseless and undistinguished as some natural force."

## HENRY V AS POLITICAL THEORY

Other critics tend to appreciate *Henry V* as the culmination of *Shakespeare's* **epic** *of English history,* the **climax** of the series that began with *Richard II* and continued with *Henry IV* parts I and II. These critics see in the four plays an overall approach to history that supports the Elizabethan concept of a social order dependent on the inviolable authority of the king. The greatest evil, according to Shakespeare's concept of history, is insurrection and civil war. Because Henry IV usurped the throne from Richard II, he inevitably brought about civil wars. It was left for his son, Henry V, innocent of Richard's blood, to achieve glory for England by defeating France.

One of the chief exponents of the **epic** theory of Shakespeare's history plays, of which *Henry V* is only one, was the twentieth-century scholar E. M. W. Tillyard, who emphasized the prevalence of the belief in Elizabethan England that a strong monarch was necessary for domestic peace as well as foreign success. Tillyard found one major flaw in Shakespeare's representation of Henry's character, namely, the extraordinary change from wild young man to ideal king. This critic felt that Shakespeare was hampered by adhering to a tradition that made no dramatic sense in the play. Like Dr. Johnson, Tillyard also felt that Shakespeare tried, in vain, to reconcile the image of Henry the ideal king with the image of Henry the hearty good fellow in the final scene of the play.

Another prominent critic who appreciates *Henry V* as an **exposition** of the Elizabethan concept of social order is the contemporary Derek Traversi, who emphasizes the inevitable conflicts experienced by a King. "The king, who rightly demands unquestioning allegiance from his subjects, is first called upon to show, through the perfection of his self-control, a complete and selfless devotion to his office." Traversi explains that Henry is an ideal monarch because he is able to master his passions and to exercise self-control at all times. He suggests at the same time however, that such self-control may become a superficial veneer covering, at best, indifference and, at worst, cruelty toward other human beings. Henry has chosen to act in such a way that he will be a successful king, which means that he cannot always be a decent individual in human relationships.

A. C. Bradley, the early twentieth-century critic, was following a similar line of thought when he wrote of Henry that "we shall discover with the many fine traits a few less pleasing." One of the most conspicuous features of Henry's character, Bradley felt, was his readiness to use other people as a means to his own ends. Thus he dropped Falstaff without compunction when his former friend became a political liability. Bradley recognized that Henry's piety was partly genuine, but he insisted that it was also partly a matter of political expedience.

Among the more enthusiastic contemporary admirers of Henry as the ideal king is J. H. Walter, who insists that Shakespeare's original audience would have had only praise for such a leader. Unlike Bradley and Traversi, he finds Henry a spiritual as well as a pragmatic leader. "It is Henry's spiritual strength, his faith and moral courage which inspire and uphold his whole army. By sheer exaltation and power of spirit he compels his men to achieve the impossible."

John Dover Wilson also finds a spiritual as well as a political example in Henry. Comparing the king's faith to that of the martyrs, Wilson cites his speech before the battle of Agincourt, "And how thou pleasest, God, dispose the day," as proof of his deep-rooted faith. Ultimately it is this faith which is the justification for the war and the refutation of accusations that the war is pure aggression and morally reprehensible.

A more moderate estimate of Henry's character is offered by John Palmer, who finds that Shakespeare neither extols nor censures his **protagonist**, but simply renders his character in the drama as he found it in the chronicles. Palmer notes that Shakespeare's Henry shirks his moral responsibility by holding either his subordinates (the Archbishop) or his enemies (the French king and Dauphin) liable for the consequences of his own decision to go to war. The critic also finds that Henry's soliloquy reveals a certain childish petulance at the burdens of an office which he otherwise thoroughly enjoys. In Palmer's opinion, however, Shakespeare intended to present Henry as the kind of man who is naturally successful in political life, without judging the moral quality of the man.

## COMEDY IN HENRY V

While critical commentary has centered on the character of Henry and on the moral and political implications of the play, there has also been some controversy over the comic subplot. Comparing the level of comedy in *Henry V* with that in *Henry IV*, especially part I, many critics have felt that Shakespeare was not at his best in the later work. A particularly sore point has been the absence of Falstaff, who Shakespeare promised (at the end of *Henry IV* part II) would appear in his next play. Dr. Johnson felt that Shakespeare realized quite rightly that Falstaff would be out of place in the patriotic drama of *Henry V*, but A. C. Bradley contended that an audience that loves Falstaff cannot help but blame the king for turning him away. Other critics, particularly J. D. Wilson, have undertaken to answer this charge of Bradley's by pointing out how unsuitable Falstaff's presence would be in *Henry V*, where a serious respect for the authority of the king is the dominant **theme**. He argues moreover that Henry should not be blamed for rejecting Falstaff for the sake of the kingship. Devotion to country is a higher ideal than faithfulness in friendship with a merry rascal, even if he is as lovable as Falstaff.

Another opinion on the subject of Falstaff was first offered by H. D. Gray, who suggested that Shakespeare was forced to drop Falstaff from *Henry V* when Will Kempe, the actor who formerly played that comic part, left the repertory company in 1599 while Shakespeare was writing the play. As evidence, Gray cited the stage directions "Enter Will" included in the early Quarto edition of the play. Most critics, however, evaluate the Falstaff question in terms of dramatic propriety rather than practical expediency.

O. J. Campbell suggests that the low-life scenes were not in the play originally but added later, giving as evidence the perfunctory way in which the prologue had been adjusted to accommodate a reference.

# HENRY V

## ESSAY QUESTIONS AND ANSWERS

Question: Why was Henry V a particularly significant king for Elizabethan England?

Answer: Queen Elizabeth resembled Henry V in the nature of her achievements both at home and abroad and in the extreme devotion she was able to elicit from her subjects. Shakespeare's audiences would naturally notice striking similarities between these two strong monarchs.

In the course of the play, mention is made of the civil wars that ravaged the peace of England during the reigns of Richard II and Henry IV. Unlike his predecessors, Henry was able to win the loyalty of his Welsh, Irish, and Scots as well as English subjects. Queen Elizabeth's reign was also known for the prevalence of internal peace, although she had difficulties with Ireland to which reference is made in the fifth act of the play. Although Elizabeth was not, like Henry, born in Wales, her grandfather, Henry VII, founder of the Tudor dynasty, was from Wales, and Elizabeth made the most of her Welsh connections. If Henry in his dealings with Fluellen and others shows himself as a good fellow, popular with the commons, Elizabeth was not behind him in this respect. Whereas he was known affectionately as Henry, she was fondly called "good Queen Bess."

On the international scene, Queen Elizabeth brought England to a new position of importance. In 1588 the Spanish Armada, representing the armed might of the most powerful nation in Europe, undertook an invasion of England. The English fleet, in one of the most celebrated battles in naval history, defeated the Spanish Armada despite the seemingly impossible odds. This great English victory bears a striking resemblance to the battle of Agincourt, for in both cases the English were expected to lose and in both cases, inspired by a heroic monarch, they won.

In many ways England under Henry V was very different from England under Elizabeth, but Shakespeare chose to attribute to Henry and his followers the spirit in Renaissance England of fierce patriotism. Nationalism, historically, was practically unknown in the early fifteenth century, but the words and deeds of King Henry V fitted in perfectly with the Elizabethan concept of an ideal monarch, devoted to the needs and aspirations of the nation-state.

Question: In what ways are Pistol and Fluellen similar, and in what ways are they different?

Answer: Pistol and Fluellen are both comic characters: both have distinctive speech patterns involving a certain grandiloquence, and both love to hear the sound of their own voices. Pistol specializes in **alliteration** and bombast, while Fluellen likes to bring the conversation around to ancient heroes, even though he has a very vague idea of history, and his logic leaves much to be desired.

Essentially, however, they are very different. Pistol is a rogue and a coward, who came to France for one thing only, booty. He has no concept of personal honor and no concern for the fate of his country. He thinks the king is a fine fellow, but he has no intention of risking his life for him. The fact that he captures a French prisoner in no way diminishes his cowardice. Fluellen, on the other hand, is a national, heroic type, although presented in familiar and even comic terms. He is dead serious about the war and is a gallant soldier who is honored to be able to run extra risks for his sovereign. His concept of obedience and discipline is very strict. When Pistol asks him to intervene on behalf of Bardolph, Fluellen refuses. He declares that he would not try to alter the course of justice even for the sake of his own broth. Fluellen is a man of principle. When the two men meet in <u>Act V, Scene 1</u>, the difference between them becomes very clear. Pistol talks about making Fluellen eat his leek, but the Welshman actually forces Pistol to do just that. Pistol just talks; Fluellen acts. At the end of this scene Pistol resolves to return to England as a thief. It is not revealed what Fluellen will do, but there is no doubt that he will follow an honorable calling.

Question: In what ways does Shakespeare indicate that Henry is leading a unified nation?

Answer: In the opening scene of the play the Archbishop of Canterbury declares that Henry is universally admired by all classes of society. In the second scene he assures the king that the clergy, in support of his war effort, will contribute the largest sum of money ever raised by the church for a king. In the same scene several of the nobility tell Henry that there is widespread popular approval of the war throughout the country.

The three conspirators who have plotted against the life of the king all express heartfelt repentance when their treachery is brought to light, and express gratitude to God for preventing their crime. Thus, even those men who had intended to betray the king finally wish him all success.

The four captains, Gower, Fluellen, Macmorris, and Jamy represent the four major divisions of Henry's kingdom: England, Wales, Ireland, and Scotland. Although they quarrel among themselves, they are unanimous in their loyalty to the king. Among the lower ranks of the soldiers, even Pistol expresses a strong feeling of affection for the king. The three common soldiers, Court, Bates, and Williams, are all resolved to fight lustily for the king even though as dutiful subjects they do not presume to judge the merits of his cause. Thus, throughout the army there is only devotion and courage.

Question: What is the historical explanation for the English victory over the numerically superior French army? What is the explanation suggested by the play?

Answer: Historians explain the battle of Agincourt in terms of the new and more flexible equipment used by the English. In the Middle Ages warfare was essentially hand-to-hand combat between heavily armored knights on horseback in contests of personal strength and skill. The French adhered to this traditional concept of warfare as late as 1415 at Agincourt. The English, however, relied on lightly armed long-range yeomen archers, whose arrows took a serious toll of French chevaliers before the hand-to-hand combat could begin. The muddy field at Agincourt was disastrous for the French, whose horses and heavily encumbered riders bogged down in the wet ground, providing easy targets for the English archers. This battle is of special interest to historians because it marks a turning point in military history. Henceforth, the heavily armored knight on horseback would become less and less important compared with the lightly armed long-range archer.

Shakespeare never mentions this historical explanation, although it is contained in the chronicles that were his sources. In the context of the play the English victory seems to be the result of a moral and spiritual superiority over the enemy. Both before and after Agincourt, Henry expresses his reliance on Providence to determine the outcome of the battle. No one contradicts or even modifies his statement that the victory is entirely the result of divine intervention.

In the very beginning of the play, the Archbishop of Canterbury establishes the validity of Henry's claim to the French throne, and throughout the drama the English cause is accepted as morally just while the French are in the wrong. The English have more than right on their side, they have a great leader. Henry galvanizes his army before the battle of Agincourt with his stirring appeal to honor in the Crispin Crispianus Day speech. The English consider themselves a band of brothers, a privileged group joined together in a common cause. The French lack the spirit and the motivation that plays an important part in the English victory.

Question: What is the dramatic importance of Henry's soliloquy in Act IV, Scene I?

Answer: It is the night before the battle of Agincourt. Henry has been wandering through his army camp trying to cheer the failing spirits of his men. Disguised by a cloak belonging to one of his captains and by the dark night, he has conversed with three common soldiers who raise questions about the king's responsibility towards the men whom he leads into battle.

This discussion as well as his own natural fears and concerns result in the soliloquy.

Henry is always in public and always aware that he must choose his words for the effect that they will produce. The soliloquy, however, comes straight from his heart, and we take it to be the revelation of his innermost feelings. In his talk with the three soldiers he said that he thought the king was but a man, with senses and fears and weaknesses like every other man. Now, alone, he pursues this train of thought, as he realizes that the king bears burdens of which the common man never dreams. His subjects hold him liable for their personal responsibilities: wives, children, debts, and souls. He can never trust any man for fear of being betrayed, and he can never reveal his true feelings for fear that they will be used against him or that they will undermine his authority by making him appear to the multitude like what he truly is, a mortal man. The king can never know the joys of privacy and of peace of mind, for he can never relax his vigil over the country's peace. And in return for all these burdens, the king's only compensation is "ceremony," the external pomp which brings no heart's ease, no inner tranquility.

Throughout most of the play, Henry seems entirely at home in his role as King, exceptionally well qualified to lead men and to make decisions. Yet at this crucial moment before the battle, we suddenly realize that there is a level of Henry's being that we have ignored, the private man within the public figure. And the recognition that the king is, after all, "but a man" makes him in our eyes all the more noble a figure, for we now realize that it is an effort for him to act cheerful when he is afraid, and to keep his feelings to himself. That is what a king must do, however, and Henry does it.

Question: Why does Henry woo Katherine in prose instead of verse?

Answer: Like the other characters in the main action, Henry generally speaks in **blank verse**, unrhymed iambic **pentameter**. When he woos Katherine, however, he is trying to act like an ordinary man, a plain soldier who is unaccustomed to the **conventions** of aristocratic society. When he wants to, Henry can be as regal and as formal as any man in Europe; in fact, he has just shown this when speaking to Katherine's father, the king of France. Even though politics has determined his choice of a wife, Henry prefers to woo her in a personal rather than a formal manner. If they are to live together for the rest of their lives, they may as well get to know each other as ordinary people and not as masks of royalty.

This scene has been severely attacked by critics, beginning with Samuel Johnson, who deemed it completely out of keeping with Henry's character as it is delimited in the rest of the play. Such criticism fails to appreciate the real problems of the situation. Henry is left alone, probably for the first time, with the young lady who, in all likelihood, will be his wife. What should he say to her? Either he can engage in idle chatter and avoid the subject of their future relationship (although even that is not easy because of the language problem). Or, in accordance with the demands of courtly love, he can act the role of the heartsick lover, praising his lady to the skies even though he barely knows her. Or, finally, he can refuse to take himself or the situation too seriously. This, in fact, is what he does; by dispraising himself to her and by refusing to declare that he will die of love if she rejects his suit, he actually stands the best chance of winning her approval for his lack of affectation, his directness, modesty, and gay good spirits.

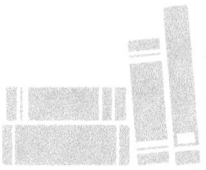

# HENRY V

## SUBJECT BIBLIOGRAPHY AND GUIDE TO RESEARCH PAPERS

A research paper depends, first of all, on the use of an authoritative text. There are many excellent editions of *Henry V* including helpful notes and introductions. Among the best of these are the volumes in the *Yale Shakespeare* (New Haven, 1918) with notes by Robert D. French; the *Arden Shakespeare* (Cambridge, Mass., 1954), edited by J. H. Walter; the *Pelican Shakespeare* (Baltimore, 1957), edited by L. B. Wright and V. L. Freund; and the *Laurel Shakespeare* (New York, 1962), edited by Francis Fergusson.

Research material on the play and on Shakespeare can be divided into the following categories:

### SOURCES OF HENRY V

*Chief Pre-Shakespearean Dramas,* ed. Joseph Quincy Adams. Boston, 1924. In this anthology is the text of the *Famous Victories of Henry V,* an earlier play on the same subject. It is interesting to compare the way in which Shakespeare and his predecessor handled the same material.

Holinshed's *Chronicle as Used in Shakespeare's Plays*, ed. Allardyce and Josephine Nicoll, New York, 1927. The part of Holinshed's *Chronicle* that Shakespeare made use of in *Henry V* is contained in this volume.

## ORIGINAL TEXT

*The First Folio of Shakespeare's Plays*, in a Fascimile Edition, ed. Helge Kokeritz and C. T. Prouty. New Haven, 1955. This reproduction of the First Folio edition of Shakespeare's plays gives an idea of the spelling and punctuation in the sixteenth century.

## CRITICISM OF HENRY V

Bradley, A. C. *Oxford Lectures on Poetry.* Oxford, 1902. Contains an evaluation of the character of Henry, with emphasis on the omission of Falstaff and the relevance of this omission to the play as a whole.

Hazlitt, William. *Characters of Shakespeare's Plays.* London, 1870. The Romantic approach to *Henry V,* extremely critical of the play.

Johnson, Samuel. *On Shakespeare,* ed. Walter Raleigh. Oxford, 1908. A few pages of insights into the play; adversely critical only of the last act.

Masefield, John. *Shakespeare.* London, 1911. An interesting analysis of the character of the king.

Palmer, John. *Political Characters of Shakespeare.* London, 1948. An excellent analysis of the character of the king, the structure of the play, and summary of diverse critical opinion on the subject.

Traversi, Derek. *An Approach to Shakespeare.* New York, 1956. A brief and not startling appraisal of the play.

Wilson, J. D. *The Fortunes of Falstaff Cambridge,* 1953. Mainly dealing with the character of Falstaff in the earlier Shakespearean history plays, Wilson devoted a few interesting pages to the fate of this comic character in *Henry V.*

Van Doren, Mark. *Shakespeare.* New York, 1953. This modern poet and scholar has some very harsh words for *Henry V,* which he considers one of the weakest plays of Shakespeare's middle period.

# HENRY V

## GENERAL BIOGRAPHY AND CRITICISM

Alexander, P., *Shakespeare's Life and Art,* New York, 1961. Development of Shakespeare from apprentice to mature artist.

Brooks, C., "Shakespeare as a symbolist poet," *Yale Rev.*, June, 1945.

Chambers, E. K., *The Elizabethan Stage,* Oxford, 1923. A classic for the study of Shakespeare's stage problems.

Coleridge, S. T., *Shakespearean Criticism,* reprint, New York, 1961. An interesting study of the play from a nineteenth century critic's viewpoint.

Farnham, Willard, *Medieval Heritage of Elizabethan Tragedy,* New York, 1956. One of the most complete studies of the classical vs. medieval concept of tragedy. Excellent comments on *King Richard III.*

Goddard, Harold, *The Meaning of Shakespeare,* New York.

Green, V. H. H., *The Later Plantagenets,* London, 1955. Shows the weakness of the line that accounts for their fall from power.

Hazlitt, Wm., *Characters of Shakespeare's Plays,* modern reprint. Thinks *King Richard III* is better on the stage than read in quiet, as was then being urged by some.

Hughes, A. E., *Shakespeare and His Welsh Characters.* Interesting comments on the Duke of Richmond and his Welsh background.

Perry, Alice I., *Stage History of Shakespeare's King Richard The Third,* New York, 1909. This work gives a full account of the various acting editions of the play.

Rowse, A. L., *William Shakespeare,* New York, 1963. Gives an excellent re-evaluation of the critics' views on *King Richard III.*

Sprague, A. C., *Shakespearean Players and Performances,* Cambridge, 1954. An account of the late sixteenth century stage.

## GENERAL: CLASSIC CRITICISM AND INTERPRETATION

Bradley, A. C. "Shakespeare's *Antony and Cleopatra*" in *Oxford Lectures on Poetry.* London, 1950.

Case, R. H. and M. R. Ridley. *Introduction to the Arden edition of Antony and Cleopatra.* Cambridge, Mass., 1955.

Chambers, E. K. *Shakespeare: A Survey.* London, 1925.

Charney, Maurice. *Shakespeare's Roman Plays.* Cambridge, Mass., 1961.

Coleridge, S. T. *Notes and Lectures upon Shakespeare.* London, 1849, V. I, 145-148.

Danby, John F. *Poets on Fortune's Hill.* London, 1952.

Dickey, Franklin M. *Not Wisely, But Too Well.* San Marino, Calif., 1957.

Dowden, Edward. *Shakespeare.* N. Y., 1881.

Dryden, John. *Preface to All for Love in Mermaid Series.* London, 1949-50

Farnham, Willard. *Shakespeare's Tragic Frontier.* Berkeley, Calif., 1950.

Granville-Barker, Harley. *Prefaces to Shakespeare.* Princeton, N. J., 1952, V. I.

Hazlitt, William. *Characters of Shakespeare's Plays.* London, 1957.

Holzknecht, Karl J. *The Background of Shakespeare's Plays.* N. Y., 1950.

Johnson, Samuel. *Samuel Johnson on Shakespeare* (ed. W. K. Wimsatt, Jr.). N. Y., 1960.

Knight, G. Wilson. *The Imperial **Theme**.* London, 1951.

Knights, Lionel C. *Some Shakespearean Themes.* Stanford, Calif., 1960.

Mac Callum, M. W. *Shakespeare's Roman Plays.* London, 1910.

Mack, Maynard. *Introduction to the Pelican edition of Antony and Cleopatra.* Baltimore, 1960.

Ribner, Irving. *Patterns in Shakespearean Tragedy.* N. Y., 1960.

Rosen, William. *Shakespeare and the Craft of Tragedy.* Cambridge, Mass., 1960.

Spencer, T. J. B. *Shakespeare: The Roman Plays.* London, 1963.

Spurgeon, Caroline. *Shakespeare's **Imagery**.* Boston, 1958.

Symons, Arthur. "*Antony and Cleopatra,*" in *Studies in the Elizabethan Drama.* London, 1920.

Traversi, D. A. *Approach to Shakespeare.* London, 1938.

Van Doren, Mark. *Shakespeare,* N. Y., 1939.

Wilson, Harold S. *On the Design of Shakespearean Tragedy.* Toronto, 1957.

Readings In Critical Methods as Applied to Shakespeare

Auerbach, Erich, *Mimesis* (1953), Ch. 13, "The Weary Prince" (Prince Hal in *Henry IV,* Part Two).

Brooks, Cleanth, The *Well-Wrought Urn* (1947), Ch. 2, "The Naked Babe and the Cloak of Manliness," (a study of **imagery** in *Macbeth*).

Downer, Alan S., "The Life of Our Design: The Function of **Imagery** in the Poetic Drama," in *Shakespeare: Modern Essays in Criticism,* ed. Leonard Dean (1957).

Empson, William, *The Structure of Complex Words* (1951), chapters on "Fool in *Lear,*" and "Honest in *Othello.*"

Fergusson, Francis, *The Human Image in Dramatic Literature* (1957), Part II, "Shakespeare."

\_\_\_\_*The Idea of a Theatre* (1949), Ch. 4, "'*Hamlet,* Prince of Denmark;' The Analogy of Action."

Granville-Barker, *Harley On Dramatic Method* (1956), Ch. 3, "Shakespeare's Progress."

Kitto, H. D. F., *Form and Meaning in Drama* (1956), Ch. 9 "*Hamlet.*"

## LIFE AND TIMES OF SHAKESPEARE

Chute, Marchette. *Shakespeare of London.* New York, 1956. A very interesting biography that also provides analysis of Shakespeare's world.

Halliday, F. E. *Shakespeare: A Pictorial Biography.* New York, 1956. Excellent pictures.

Fluchere, Henri. *Shakespeare and the Elizabethans.* New York, 1956. Relates Shakespeare to the other dramatists of his time and to the world in which they lived.

Spencer, Theodore. *Shakespeare and the Nature of Men.* New York, 1951. A discussion of the philosophical background of Shakespeare's England with particular emphasis on man's place in nature.

Trevelyan, G. M. *History of England, Volume II: The Tudors and the Stuart Era.* New York, 1953. A good account of the history of Tudor England.

Tillyard, E. M. *The Elizabethan World Picture.* New York, 1944. An excellent description of the concepts, attitudes, and manners in Shakespearean England, supplying important background material for the understanding of all Shakespeare's work.

## SHAKESPEAREAN THEATER PRODUCTION

Adams, John Cranford. *The Globe Playhouse: Its Design and Equipment.* New York, 1942.

De Banke, Cecile. *Shakespearean Production, Then and Now. A Manual for the Scholar Player.* New York, 1953.

Hodges, C. Walter. *The Globe Restored.* New York, 1954.

Smith, Irwin. *Shakespeare's Globe Playhouse. A Modern Reconstruction in Text and Scale Drawings.* New York, 1956.

These books describe the ways in which Shakespeare's plays were originally produced, and De Banke's account includes helpful suggestions for the modern producer.

## SHAKESPEARE'S HISTORY PLAYS

Campbell, Lily B. *Shakespeare's Histories: Mirrors of Elizabethan Policy.* San Marino, California, 1947. An excellent description of the development of historiography in the English Renaissance, with a separate chapter on *Henry V* analyzed as the ideal victorious king.

Chambers E. K. *Shakespeares A Survey.* New York, 1959. A collection of essays on various Shakespeare plays, including an excellent chapter on *Henry V* in relation to patriotism in sixteenth century England.

Holzknecht, Karl J. *The Backgrounds of Shakespeare's Plays.* New York, 1950. A particularly useful account of the role of chroniclers and writers of popular history works for the theater in Tudor England. Shakespeare is seen in perspective with other men also concerned with historical themes.

Schelling, R. E. *The English Chronicle Play.* New York, 1902. An interesting discussion of the **genre** of the chronicle play flourishing before and during Shakespeare's lifetime.

Tillyard, E. M. W. *Shakespeare's History Plays.* London, 1956. An analysis of the myth of the Tudor Monarchy and the men who celebrated it in chronicle and drama, including Shakespeare. There is an excellent chapter on *Henry V* in this connection.

Traversi, Derek. *From Richard II to Henry V* Stanford, California, 1957. An exploration of the dominant **themes** in Shakespeare's **epic** of English history, with an interesting chapter emphasizing the moral development of the character of Henry V.

www.ingramcontent.com/pod-product-compliance
Lightning Source LLC
LaVergne TN
LVHW011710060526
838200LV00051B/2851